Appraising Teacher Performance

Appraising Teacher Performance

James Lewis, Jr.

Associate Professor
Villanova University
Villanova, Pa.

Parker Publishing Company, Inc.
West Nyack, N.Y.

Library of Congress Cataloging in Publication Data

Lewis, James Jr. (Date)
    Appraising teacher performance.
    Bibliography: p.
    1. Teachers, Rating of. I. Title.
LB2838.L43   371.1'44   72-10155
ISBN 0-13-043661-5

Printed in the United States of America

**To my late grandmother,
Laura Arnold Wilkerson**

Also by the author:

- *A Contemporary Approach to Nongraded Education*
- *Administering the Individualized Instruction Program*
- *Differentiating the Teaching Staff*

Foreword

Few of us actively engaged in the education of children today enjoy the satisfaction of knowing that parents and taxpayers are really sold on what we are accomplishing. With today's public focus on accountability, we are giving renewed attention to that thorniest of problems —teacher appraisal—in the hope of changing this discouraging situation. I believe that James Lewis, Jr. has gotten to the heart of this problem and presents in this book a constructive and practical solution.

To date most of us have known only conflict and frustration in dealing with teacher appraisal. Pressed by anxious boards of education to "get tough" in appraising teachers, school administrators have braced themselves for a renewal of the historic, even international, animosity between teachers and administrators. Teachers have condemned administrators and boards for lowering teacher morale. And none of us has had much confidence that, for all this social cost, better teaching has really resulted.

To remedy this situation Dr. Lewis proposes, first of all, that we abandon the comparative rating of teachers—a startling proposal, indeed! Once you seriously consider this possibility, though, you begin to realize how much we might gain by such a move. The principal need no longer be in the position of establishing a definitive, unchallengeable and computer-like assessment of each teacher, vulnerable to the usual teacher charge of insufficient evidence or lack of adequate expertise on the part of the principal. He need no longer pose as one having the wisdom of Solomon at his command or one whose status in the educational hierarchy somehow renders his opinion as a generalist automatically superior to that of the teacher specialist. We rule out this adversary relationship.

Instead the administrator simply aims to establish agreement with the teacher on whether or not the teacher's performance meets local expectancies—including the teacher's own. The teacher's self-esteem and right to his own professional opinion are preserved. The task is to negotiate a meeting of the minds.

This book further proposes that we substitute a focus on teacher improvement for the old focus on teacher shortcomings. Beginning and ending with the teacher's self-appraisal, the assessment process concentrates on agreed-upon areas for improvement: improvement of the school and, for this purpose, improvement of the teacher himself. The whole procedure is based on the assumption that the teacher *will* improve if given the encouragement and the help he needs to do so. In such an atmosphere of faith and trust, improvement is far more likely than in the atmosphere of fear and coercion fostered by the conventional approach, with its ideal of perfection and its emphasis on shortcomings from this ideal. And in such a supportive atmosphere the promotion of teacher cooperation and the tailoring of in-service education to serve the individual teacher's needs can be very natural outcomes.

Granted, then, that teacher improvement *can* take place more readily in a supportive atmosphere, it is natural to ask whether the desired improvement *will*, in fact take place. Will a teacher's limitation of vision, his personal idiosyncrasies, his technical deficiencies really yield to change? If so, exactly what will happen to produce such changes?

Let me say, from personal experience with the author's approach, that remarkable things *do* in fact happen. To understand how this comes about one needs to recognize the three basic elements Lewis deals with in structuring the appraisal: *skill* on the job, *innovation* as a contributing member of a cooperating faculty, and *personal development* in one's chosen career. When a teacher is helped by an administrator to plan career advancement as a part of his appraisal, the strong motivation of search for greater personal identity comes into play. When a teacher's skill improvement is seen as a means to this end, general motivation is translated into terms of immediate increase in capability. And when a teacher sees that the contributions he undertakes to make toward school improvement gain him the active support of other teachers and, quite likely, of students and parents as well, the increase in job satisfaction has a "Hawthorne effect" which is a powerful stimulation to improved performance.

What, then, has Lewis done in his book? It appears to me that he has developed a learning-centered approach to teacher appraisal. In doing so he shows us how we can let teachers share the opportunity for individualized learning we are now so wisely making available to our students.

Dr. Lewis himself would say, I am sure, that he has merely taken a successful approach from the field of industrial management and applied it to the field of education. But I believe he has really done more than this. For he has looked beyond efficiency, quantitative output and compliance with authority, which may possibly be adequate concerns in the world of the production of inanimate things. He shows us how to deal, as well, with qualitative, humanistic results involving the development of human values and interests. In the end he tells us a good deal about how to make our schools the more humane, liberating institutions we know they must become.

A. Gordon Peterkin
Superintendent
School District 36
Winnetka, Illinois

The Importance of
Performance Appraisals
in Education

Researchers seem to arrive at [1] the same findings that, regardless of the technique or method employed, e.g., rating scale, self-analysis, classroom visitations, etc., few if any "facts" seem to have been reached concerning teacher and administrator effectiveness. Furthermore, no generally agreed upon method of measuring the competence of educators has been accepted and no methods of promoting growth, improvement and development have been generally adopted.

Although in the past we have been unable to objectively measure teachers' performance effectiveness, the traditional practice of "evaluating" educators continues to be a dominant feature of our schools.[2] Administrators continue the semi-annual ritual of writing narrative reports and/or checklist evaluations on teachers. These "evaluation" devices generally not only fail to measure adequately professional competence, but also actually result in alienating the relationship between the teacher and the administrator, do little or nothing for improving performance, and engender a false sense of security about the quality of professional performance in the school system.[3]

---

[1] Donald M. Medley and Harold E. Mizzel. "Measuring Classroom Behavior by Systematic Observation," *Handbook of Research on Teaching*, N. L. Gage, editor. Rand McNally & Co., Chicago, 1963, pp. 247-328.

[2] Bruce J. Biddle and William Ellena, Jr., editors. *Contemporary Research on Teacher Effectiveness*. Holt Rinehart & Winston, New York, 1964, pp. v-vi.

[3] E. Kay and J. R. P. France, Jr. "A Study of the Performance Appraisal Interview," *Behavioral Research Service, Technical Report*. University of Michigan, 1961.

The practical material in this book will help you avoid these and many other problems related to appraisal programs.

The traditional method of appraising (evaluating) the performance of educators is based on two common erroneous assumptions. *First*, the traditional performance appraisal program is based on a poor theory of human motivation, that telling an educator where he is doing a poor job will provide the necessary effective motivation to get him to improve his performance. Research has proven that this is not always the case. McGregor maintains:

> Contrast the situation in which a subordinate is evaluating his own performance relative to specific targets which he set a few months ago with the situation in which he is listening to his supervisor evaluate his performance against the supervisor's standards and objectives. The stage is set for rationalization, defensiveness, inability to understand, reactions that the superior is being unfair, or arbitrary. These are not conditions conducive to effective motivation.[4]

Second, the traditional performance appraisal program is based on the false assumption that the roles of the administrator and the teacher are compatible and that criticism in itself will bring on the necessary improvement in performance. The administrator, in evaluating the teacher, implies that the staff member needs to improve his performance in the direction of the objectives and standards of the administrator. Failure to achieve according to this expectation often leads to criticism, threat, anxiety, and a poor working relationship between the administrator and the teacher, which limits the supervisory effectiveness of the administrator's leadership. McGregor further states, "Judgments which are positive can perhaps be communicated effectively, but it is rather difficult to communicate critical judgments without generating defensiveness."[5]

In contrast to these two false assumptions, if we view the appraisal interview as a counseling opportunity, another problem becomes apparent concerning the traditional performance appraisal program. This problem stems from the fact that most appraisals include the administrator's evaluation of the teacher's personality traits and attitudes, in

---

[4] Douglas McGregor. *The Human Side of Enterprise*. McGraw-Hill Book Company, New York, 1960, p. 87.

[5] *Ibid*., p. 84.

addition to a subjective evaluation of performance. When this occurs, there is a tendency for the administrator to invade the personality of the teacher during the interview. If the intent of the interview is to counsel, then we have a very delicate situation. It is a rare administrator who is competent to practice psychotherapy during the counseling sessions; when he assumes the role of judge he cannot counsel effectively. The effective administrator who gets results is one who does not criticize but assumes a supportive role to the teacher.

Educators are usually appraised two or three times yearly. This points up another reason why the traditional method of appraising performance is an ineffectual method of getting improved performance: it provides 'feedback'' about performance sometimes as long as several weeks after the performance occurred. Change does occur as a result of feedback but most effective feedback occurs immediately (on the spot) after the performance. Educators can learn a great deal about their performance or lack of performance provided it is analyzed and discussed with them immediately within the performance environment and while all the conditions and evidence are available. The likelihood of appreciably improving performance several days after it takes place is relatively small. Again, the practical guidelines in this book should be helpful in this respect.

The present method of appraising the performance of educators in most schools in America appears to be dysfunctional and serves no useful purpose. Not only does it fall short of assessing adequately "true" performance; it also makes it impossible to take corrective action for professional growth, improvement and development. Furthermore, it has been a device used over the years to perpetuate the division between teachers and administrators.

This author is advocating a new approach to the performance appraisal and development program for educators. School management by objectives offers an unusually promising framework within which we can seek a solution to this perennial problem. This approach involves a clear and precise identification of performance objectives, the establishment of a realistic action plan for their achievement and an evaluation of performance in terms of measured results in achieving them. The process of accomplishing these steps is the basis for this book.

This new approach will involve a substantial effort to erase many of the ill-conceived practices of appraising the performance of educators. However, in the long run the program should pay high dividends in terms of an effectual appraising program for teachers, better morale, an improved communications network, and improved results on the part of educators and students.

James Lewis, Jr.

ACKNOWLEDGMENTS

The views expressed in these pages are my own. The contents of this book have been adapted from business and applied to education. These adaptions were arrived at from my own experience and from numerous books cited in the bibliography. I am particularly grateful to Professor Scott Morton and Dr. M. Scott Myers of the Alfred P. Sloan Institute of Management at Massachusetts Institute of Technology, who permitted me to attend their respective courses in Management Information for Planning and Control, and Management of Human Resources, where I discussed and synthesized my ideas to form this manuscript. I am indebted to the Westport, Connecticut, Public Schools where I visited and observed school management by objectives in action. This visit proved immensely beneficial in that it enabled me to confer with teachers, supervisors and administrators and learn about some of the problems encountered during the initial stages of implementing school management by objectives. I am indebted to Dr. Roy Fairfield, Director of Union Graduate School, Antioch College, Yellow Springs, Ohio, for his cogent remarks and assistance. I am also indebted to Dr. Fred Dippel, Assistant Superintendent of West Hempstead Public Schools, West Hempstead, New York, and Dr. A. Gordon Peterkin, Superintendent of Winnetka Public Schools, Winnetka, Illinois, who reviewed each chapter and offered me their invaluable advice. To Mrs. Helen Scully and Mrs. Daphne Mair, who assisted in the tedious editing and typing of various portions of this book at home, I extend my gratitude. Finally, my deep appreciation to Mrs. Edith Reisner, a librarian at Wyandanch School District, Wyandanch, New York, and a dear friend, who assisted me with documenting and revising previous drafts of this manuscript.

James Lewis, Jr.

Table of Contents

ONE

Two Approaches to Performance Appraisal Programs for Educators

The appraisal of an educator's performance has been identified with many titles: teacher evaluation, teacher observation, administrator and teacher's progress reporting, merit rating and, most recently, performance appraisal. However, regardless of the title used, these titles fit one meaning: the judgment by one or more educators, usually the immediate supervisor, of the manner in which another educator has been fulfilling his professional responsibilities to the school district over a specified period of time. Appraising teachers is based upon the sound basis that both administrator and teacher realize benefits from knowing how well the teacher is performing. The administrator benefits from having a current record of teacher's effectiveness in order to make intelligent decisions concerning tenure and promotion. The teacher is in a better position to develop his abilities when he knows when he performs well, when he does not perform well, and how he needs to develop to become more valuable to himself and the school system.

Thus, for training and development, the performance appraisal program usually consists of two significant stages: 1) understanding the performance appraisal, and 2) communicating the results. Although this process sounds relatively easy, it has become rather difficult and at times delicate. Administrators for the most part have not been able to conduct the performance appraisal well. The intent of this chapter is to highlight a new approach to per-

formance appraisal by focusing on various methods of performance appraisal, explaining the "trait" approach and the "result"
approach, elaborating on the post-appraisal conference, and expound-
ing on criticism vs. coaching and counseling as a means for improving
performance.

IDENTIFYING DIFFERENT METHODS OF PERFORMANCE APPRAISAL PROCESS

There have been many methods used in evaluating performance.[1]
Checklists are used in many schools, with the administrator checking
off in an abstract mechanical manner the items that describe the
teacher's performance. In an effort to involve the administrator more
thoughtfully, an open-ended questionnaire has been used in some
school systems; the administrator completes statements concerning the
teacher's performance on the job. In the critical-incident method which
is used in some schools for the purpose of evaluating administrators,
supervising administrators record at regular intervals the performance
of their staff members in specific situations that are considered crucial
to the successful overall performance.

In many schools across the country, a rating scale is used. The
administrator marks along a scale the degree to which, in his opinion,
a teacher demonstrates one or more performance characteristics. Therefore on a five point scale, a teacher may receive a five (highest rating)
for "enthusiasm" but be rated only two in "judgment." No evaluation
system is entirely foolproof. Most rating systems have one common
fault. Some administrators demonstrate an unintentional bias in their
ratings; they tend to rate everyone at the two extremes, a very low
or very high. This makes it very difficult to compare one administrator's
rating with that of another. To relieve the problem of unintentional
bias on the part of the administrator, some schools have added forced
distribution and forced-choice techniques to the rating procedure.

However, regardless of the specific evaluation method used, there
are two general avenues [2] by which the performance appraisal program

---

[1] For further information of various approaches to performance appraisal, refer to studies
in PERSONNEL POLICY NO. 121, APPRAISAL OF PERFORMANCE, A Research
Report from the Conference Board, New York, N.Y., 1951.

[2] Developing Management Competence: Changing Concepts and Merging Practices, Personnel
Policy No. 189," a research paper from the Conference Board, New York, N.Y. 1964, p.
29.

for educators can be arrived at. The first avenue is identified as the "trait" approach. The total performance of a teacher or administrator is reviewed and evaluated in terms of the traits or personality and operating methods that characterize his work. The second avenue is identified as the "result" approach; performance is reviewed and evaluated in terms of the specific results the educator has achieved in relation to the objectives developed for his job.

THE "TRAIT" APPROACH

The "trait" approach is based on the assumption that once an educator becomes familiar with his job, he tends to develop an individual style, or a characteristic way of performing in his area of responsibility. His teaching or administrative style is determined partially by his personality and partially by the specific responsibilities assigned to him. For example, a teacher may develop his lesson plans with great care or he may be overly-conservative in his lesson plans. An administrator may be dictatorial in his leadership style or he may be observed frequently practicing the participatory decision-making process. Few educators display extreme characteristics; there are seldom "complete devils" or "perfect angels" in any school system. However, almost all educators show both traits and habits that typify their individual styles of performance.

These traits can have a significant effect on the teacher's ability to teach and the administrator's abilities to administrate. Thus, the "trait" approach to performance appraisal focuses on the teaching and administrative characteristics as a personal basis for reviewing and assessing an educator's performance.

The initial phase of the "trait" approach to a performance appraisal program usually takes place before the program is put into operation. Administrators and teachers determine various traits which will be used as the criteria for judging teachers' and administrators' effectiveness. Forms are prepared identifying and defining the various criterion traits. Usually provision is made for a scale rating of each trait. Instructions for evaluating the "trait" approach are provided either as part of the appraisal forms or in a policy and procedure statement. An example of the "trait" approach for appraising the performance of teachers is illustrated in Figure 1-1. During the "trait" appraisal, an administrator observes the performance of a teacher and evaluates it against the criterion traits.

UNION FREE SCHOOL DISTRICT NO. 1
171 Ralph Avenue, Babylon, N. Y.

TEACHER EVALUATION FORM

		Poor	Fair	Ave.	Good	Superior
I	Adjustment to other teachers	1	2	3	4	5
II	Cooperation with all faculty	1	2	3	4	5
III	Loyalty to school	1	2	3	4	5
IV	Dependability in assignments	1	2	3	4	5
V	Effectiveness of personal relations	1	2	3	4	5
VI	Physical health and energy	1	2	3	4	5
VII	General appearance	1	2	3	4	5
VIII	Amenable to criticism	1	2	3	4	5
IX	Acts on criticisms	1	2	3	4	5
X	Pupil relationships	1	2	3	1	5
XI	Classroom management	1	2	3	4	5
XII	Teaching techniques	1	2	3	4	5
XIII	Subject-matter background	1	2	3	4	5
XIV	Professional Growth	1	2	3	4	5
XV	Emotional stability	1	2	3	4	5
XVI	Extra curricular activities	1	2	3	4	5
XVII	Clerical aspects of work	1	2	3	4	5
XVIII	All-around good influence on pupils	1	2	3	4	5
XIX	Discipline and control	1	2	3	4	5
XX	Cultural status	1	2	3	4	5

Composite rating average:

Signature of Rater: _____

Date _____

Figure 1-1 TEACHER EVALUATION FORM—THE "TRAIT" APPROACH

In some schools, a group of educators comprising either teachers and/or administrators conducts the performance review. Some appraisal report forms provide space for the evaluator to denote explanations to amplify the rating that he gives. Usually, an overall rating of the educator's performance is required from the evaluator.

In most schools the administrator discusses the appraisal reports in a conference with the teachers by commenting on the strengths and weaknesses of the performance. Each weakness is usually sandwiched between a strength. Once the administrator has discussed the entire report with the teacher, the report is signed by the administrator and teacher. A copy is kept by the administrator and placed in the teacher's file and a copy is retained by the teacher.

THE "RESULTS" APPROACH

The "results" approach, better identified as an objective-centered performance appraisal approach is based on the following rationale. An administrator or teacher is supposed to achieve certain performance objectives. All his efforts should be directed toward getting specific results that are consistent with the school district's philosophy, policies, procedures, broad educational goals and long range goals and short range objectives.

Personality traits and operating methods are important only as they affect the results achieved. Thus, an educator's performance can be reviewed and evaluated more meaningfully because his results are compared to the objectives which he has set for himself.

The initial phase of the "result" performance appraisal approach begins before the program has begun. This phase is the objective setting stage of school management by objectives. An administrator and teacher jointly determine specific objectives the teacher will be expected to achieve for the ensuing school year. Usually, there will only be six objectives; however, they should account for the teacher's major responsibilities. If the teacher achieves his objectives in accord with the school district's policies, procedures and plans, he will have contributed his share to the overall success of the school district. An example of an appraisal form used to record results is illustrated in Figure 1-2.

THE WESTPORT PUBLIC SCHOOLS
and TDR Associates

PROFESSIONAL DEVELOPMENT AND APPRAISALS PROGRAM

GOAL ACTIVITIES RECORD FORM

Pilot Project, 1969-70

TO BE COMPLETED DURING THE GOAL SETTING CONFERENCE:

Staff member's name _____

School and/or dept. _____

Staff member's role _____

Supervisor's name _____

Date that goal was set _____

Approximate date of final   Time span
assessment conference _____   for goal
                                                   attainment _____ months

Check one:

       ( )   Teaching skills goal

       ( )   Consultative/supervisory skills goal

       ( )   Program goal

       ( )   Personal goal

TO BE COMPLETED DURING FINAL ASSESSMENT CONFERENCE:

Check one:

       ( )   Did not meet goal

       ( )   Met or surpassed goal

Signatures:

     Staff member _____

     Supervisor _____

     Date _____

TEACHER EVALUATION FORM – THE "RESULT" APPROACH

Figure 1-2 TEACHER EVALUATION FORM—THE
"RESULT" APPROACH

WRITE A BRIEF DESCRIPTION OF EACH OF THE FOLLOWING. *

1. GOAL:

2. CRITERIA FOR ASSESSING DEGREE OF GOAL ATTAINMENT:

3. ROLE OF STAFF MEMBER FOR GOAL ATTAINMENT:

4. ROLE OF SUPERVISOR FOR GOAL ATTAINMENT:

5. MODIFICATIONS MADE DURING INTERIM CONFERENCES (include dates):

6. ADDITIONAL COMMENTS:

* Use and attach additional paper if necessary

Westport and TDR Associates

Malcolm P. McNair, Jr. comments on the importance of the objective setting phase of the appraisal program:

> The entire system is dependent on careful definition of job *objectives* which we have defined as the critical . . . accomplishments required of the *administrator* in a particular period if his component is to make the necessary contribution to the five-year plans of the *organization*.
>
> Some of the guidelines we use in *objective* setting are these:
>
> The *administrator's objectives* must be drafted before the *teacher's*. Then these *objectives* are integrated, as necessary, with the *teacher's* drafts. This provides the central goals to which all *teachers'* results contribute. The *administrator's* objectives are not just a collection of *teachers' objectives*, they are the synthesis . . .
>
> *Objectives* should be broad in scope and limited in number—five or six is the normal maximum. Long lists usually include the detailed *objectives* of *teachers*, not of the *administrator* himself.
>
> *Objectives* should tie directly into the school planning, budgeting process—preliminary *objectives* should be established prior to budget preparation and represent necessary progress toward division five-year objectives. Then the budget consolidates and documents in financial terms the *objectives* of all components of the division. The budgeting process may reveal inconsistencies among *objectives* of various departments or a need to modify objectives up or down. After budgets have been accepted, individual job *objectives* can be adjusted as necessary and authorized . . .
>
> *Objectives* must be harmonious within any one component and between components—objectives must be cross-checked . . . Are staff *objectives* established in support of line? Are lower levels tied in with levels above? Are short range *objectives* compatible with long range goals? . . .
>
> *Objectives* should include: specific statement of the long range goal, interim progress points and action programs, and target dates for various steps.
>
> This list of guidelines isn't exhaustive. We could go into various refinements. But it gives an impression of what is involved in the first important step, setting job *objectives*.[3]

---

[3] Taken from a Conference Board speech and printed in the *Management Record*, 1961. The author has substituted the word *objective* for *targets*, *administrator* for *manager*, *plans*

The objectives which the teacher sets for himself become part of the controls against which the teacher appraises his performance. These objectives also become the standards and the success criteria against which the teacher's performance will be evaluated during the post appraisal conference.

Making the appraisal using the result approach is much easier than using the trait approach. The administrator merely makes a comparison between the results achieved and the anticipated results, as revealed by the minimal level of acceptable performance. In this case, the administrator determines whether the teacher achieved his objective as planned, exceeded his plans, or was below plan. If the objectives are not stated in observable terms, the basic appraisal data will be virtually useless.

The administrator must also consider the performance made by the teacher. If the teacher exceeded his objectives, was it at the expense of policies and procedures? Were the objectives realistically low? Were these challengeable objectives? However, on the other hand, if the teacher did not reach his objectives, were they set too high? Were appropriate motivational techniques "applied" to get improved performance? Did the teacher's personality or methods prevent the successful achievement of the objectives? Was the action plan satisfactorily and adequately constructed?

The administrator must consider the above questions because the appraisal is the beginning of the initial stage of planning and setting objectives. By understanding the reason for performance during the present year or period of performance, regardless of its outcome, it is possible for the administrator and the teacher to plan and set objectives for the remaining year or period with greater confidence for successful obtainment.

THE POST APPRAISAL CONFERENCE

For the purpose of developing either administrators or teachers, the most significant phase of the performance appraisal program, whether using either the trait or results approach, may not be the observation of the educator's performance but rather what is accomplished in the post appraisal conference between the educator and his immediate supervisor.

---

for *profit goals, organization* for *division, teacher's* for *subordinate's* and *school* for *business* in the original text of Malcolm P. McNair, Jr.

One purpose of the conference is to inform the educator as to what he has achieved in terms of what he was expected to achieve. Equally important, the post appraisal conference is expected to lead to concrete suggestions and recommendations for improving performance where it has been weak and for the further development of strength where it has been satisfactory. When this type of planning takes place successfully during the conference, it is said to be the major contribution that the results appraisal program makes to developing administrators and teachers. Once a school makes the transition from the trait approach to results approach it will be necessary for administrators to receive extensive workshop training in effective conference techniques.

Both the teacher and administrator should prepare for the post appraisal conference by thoroughly reviewing the appraisal report form. In some schools, the form is completed by the teacher; in other schools, the form is completed by the administrator. It is recommended that plenty of uninterrupted time be allowed for the conference. This may necessitate conducting the conference in a private setting of the school. During the conference, the administrator tries to put the teacher at ease and encourage him to express his views as to why his performance was above, on, and below plan. Usually, the performance appraisal report is used as the agenda. During some conferences, however, there may be only a general discussion covering performance, usually to bring out a specific point.

The post appraisal conference is an ideal time for clearing up any grievances. Disagreement concerning some phase of an educator's performance can be discussed and resolved. Differing viewpoints and ideas can also be brought up for discussion and reconciled. Usually, before the conference is terminated, a follow-up conference date is mutually agreed upon for reviewing the next period of performance. Whenever the post appraisal conference is executed effectively, it provides an opportunity for the administrator to chart a development and training course for the educator. Motivation is also an important feature of the post appraisal conference between the administrator and the teacher.

CRITICISM VS. COACHING AND COUNSELING FOR IMPROVING PERFORMANCE

One of the significant differences between the trait approach and the results approach to appraisal lies within the post appraisal conference. In the trait approach, the conference between the administrator and teacher usually takes the form of critical review of a teacher's performance. Although the administrator is often told to make constructive criticism, this is not usually the case. Three researchers cite some interesting observations about criticism during the performance appraisal conference at a General Electric plant.

> The average subordinate reacted defensively to seven of the manager's criticisms during the appraisal interview (that is, he reacted defensively about 54% of the time when criticized). Denial of shortcomings cited by the manager, blaming others and various other forms of excuses were recorded by the observers as defensive reactions.
>
> Constructive responses to criticism were rarely observed. In fact, the average was less than one per interview. Not too surprising, along with this, was the finding that the more criticism a man received in the performance appraisal discussion, the more defensively he reacted. Men who received an above-average number of criticisms showed more than five times as much defensive behavior as those who received a below-average number of criticisms. Subordinates who received a below-average number of criticisms, for example, reacted defensively only about one time out of three. But those who received an above-average number reacted defensively almost two times out of three.[4]

The author speculates that these results would most likely be true of teachers who are appraised by "constructive critical" administrators. The researcher further established, " . . . it does appear clear that frequent criticism constitutes so strong a threat to self-esteem that it disrupts rather than improves subsequent performance."[5]

To "coat" critical comments of performance most administrators usually start off the conference by complimenting the teacher, reserving criticism for the last part of the conference.

When the "results" approach to appraisal is implemented, the most human part of the program should, in all probability, occur when the administrator and teacher discuss job performance during the post appraisal conference. It is at this time that the administrator assumes the role of a coach and counselor instead of one who merely criticizes

---

[4] H. H. Meyer, F. Kay and J. R. P. French, Jr. "Split Role In Performance Appraisal," *Harvard Business Review*, January-February, 1965, pp. 125-126.

[5] *Ibid*.

to get improved performance. Let it not be said that criticism has no place in the conference, for a good coach will not only criticize but will also provide a stream of instructions, comments, questions, suggestions and constructive feedback to motivate the teacher to improve performance. The effective administrator is one who recognizes that the manner in which he would teach, instruct, motivate, assist, etc., may not be the best way for the teacher. There are many ways to perform a number of things and what may work for one may not work or even fit the style of another. Proper coaching and counseling permits an educator to try out different approaches and techniques so that he may learn from experience what works best for his students and himself. Therefore, the coach and counselor might recommend the results to be expected, but may not suggest the activities or method. The administrator may observe something going wrong in the teacher's classroom, but may question the teacher about it rather than order him to change. The question posed by the administrator might help the teacher to locate and understand the source of the difficulty because of a lack of information. Perhaps the most important part to realize is that the teacher is led to discuss and correct matters to improve his performance himself, so that he has an understanding of the performance outcome. Except when problem-solving objectives become necessary, the administrator keeps interference to a minimum in order to give the teacher a chance to determine and correct his mistakes to get improved performance.

SUMMARY

The performance appraisal program consists of two important stages: understanding the performance and communicating the results. There are many methods used in evaluating performance. Checklists are used in many schools. In some schools a rating scale is used. There are two avenues for implementing a performance appraisal program. The first avenue is the "trait" approach which is used in most schools in the country. In this approach, the teacher and the administrator's performance is reviewed and evaluated in terms of traits or personality and operating methods that characterize his work. The second avenue is identified as the "results" approach, more appropriately known as the objective-centered approach. Through this approach an educator's performance is evaluated in terms of objectives which he has set for himself. The post appraisal conference is to inform the educator as to what he has achieved in terms of what he was expected to achieve. Neither the "trait" nor the "results" approach in itself will guarantee an effective performance appraisal program for educators. However, there is strong evidence to support the case that when the "trait" approach to appraisal is implemented, there is a tendency to weigh performance too heavily on personality without clear direction for measuring result. Whenever the results approach to performance appraisal is implemented, the objectives are more apt to be achieved because the modification, revision or deletion of plans during the conference are part of the overall plans for reaching the objectives. Criticism does little to improve performance; in fact, in some cases it actually resulted in retrogression in performance. Coaching and counseling which is an integral phase of the "results" approach to performance appraisal is an effective method of motivating educators to improve performance.

TWO

Implementing the Performance Appraisal Program

Implementing the objective-centered performance appraisal progam is a complex job. It will take time and the experience of others who are already familiar with the concept to implement an effective program. Perhaps the most important step towards implementing such a program is through the formation of carefully developed and comprehensive procedural guidelines for initiating the program. Whenever human beings are an integral part of a program, the success or failure of that program rests with each and every individual, each being a variable which can enhance or destroy the program. It is because of this factor that the author wishes to emphasize that any program can only be as effective as the people within that program. For this reason the implementation of the program should follow the recommendations outlined in Figure 2-1 and further delineated in this chapter. This chapter will deal primarily with precautionary measures and two approaches for introducing the objective-centered performance appraisal program.

PRECAUTIONARY MEASURES

Before proceeding with the introductory phase of an objective-centered performance appraisal program the author feels compelled to cite some precautionary measures which should be considered in order for the program to begin smoothly.

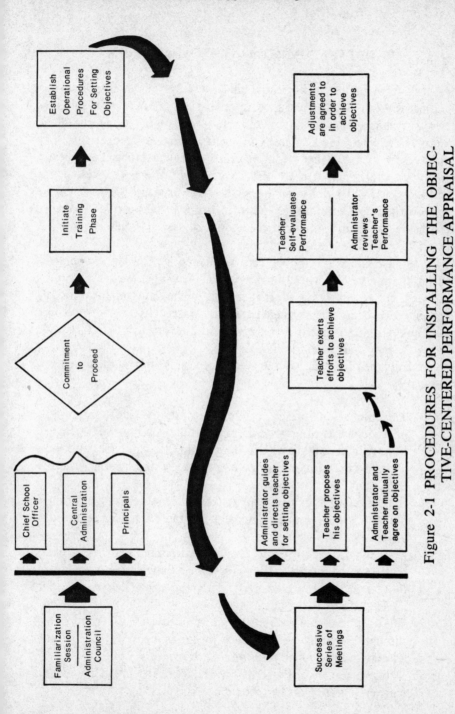

Figure 2-1 PROCEDURES FOR INSTALLING THE OBJEC-
TIVE-CENTERED PERFORMANCE APPRAISAL
PROGRAM

OBTAIN COMMITMENT FROM THE TOP

The most important condition that must be met in installing the objective-centered performance appraisal program is the support, endorsement, or permission of the top administrator in the organizational unit where the system is to be implemented. The premise that success for every teacher means helping the principal to succeed means also that the principal must be in accord with the objectives of the teachers and must not oppose the methods used by the teachers to achieve them. Therefore the place to begin installing the system is with the top administrator of the school or system where it is to be started.

The installation of the objective-centered performance appraisal program in a school district in the state of New York was successfully carried out because the superintendent, while on sabbatical leave, attended courses in management at Massachusetts Institute of Technology and decided that the system had strong possibilities for the school system where he is employed.

Usually the installation of the system proceeds through the following phases:

1. The chief school officer, central administrative staff, and principals become familiar with the concept and learn how it operates.
2. Following a commitment to the system, the chief school officer and the central administrative staff assess the school system's performance.
3. Initiate the training phase for installing the system either through the on-the-job training approach or the in-service education approach.
4. Policies are developed to classify procedures and to facilitate the implementation of the program. Changes are made from the "trait" approach to the "result" approach. Other changes as needed are also made.
5. The system of setting performance objectives is extended down through a successive series of meetings between the various administrators, supervisors and teachers.
6. Using Statement of Performance Objectives as a plan and guide, teachers exert effort to achieve objectives.

7. Teacher self-evaluates performance. Administrator evaluates teacher's performance. Teacher's performance is discussed and reviewed by administrator. Mutal agreement is reached.
8. Adjustments are made by the teacher to achieve objectives.

MINIMIZE PAPERWORK AND CLERICAL CHORES

An assurance of failure of any new program is to bog down administrators, supervisors and teachers with tons of paperwork. The most prudent administrator will develop one form for denoting performance objectives and action plans and one form for recording the performance review. Bulletins and reports should be disseminated only when necessary and an effort should be made to keep the message succinct. Clerical chores which are required to administer the program should be held to an absolute minimum consistent with adequate control.

Some school districts when implementing a new program should do so only after undertaking the program on a small scale departmentally or in a particular school. The experience gained here on a controllable scale is used as the basis for implementing the program on a district-wide basis. Some school districts have been known to implement the program district-wide at one swoop. Usually those districts use a long range plan for ironing out the problem areas in order to give all the school personnel some experience with the program. Some school districts might wish to implement the program in an area or a department, and, after a period of time (say, three to six months), extend implementation; it is advisable to have current surveillance of the program to enable solving problems which might have occurred during the implementation phase.

EXPECT REASONABLE FIRST-YEAR RESULTS

Expect only reasonable results during the first year—drastic changes from the objective-centered performance appraisal program will not be realized during the first year regardless of what plan is used. Realizing the benefits from this program is slow and gradual but inevitable progress will take place. Improvement should be seen as a long term project which will pay increased dividends over a period of years. Once administrators, supervisors and teachers begin to think and act in terms of objectives, the concept will grow and bear fruit.

Some school districts which relied too heavily on short term evaluation reports abandoned the program because a "miracle" did not occur overnight. Jay W. Forrester cautions educators on short term responses:

> . . . in complex systems the short term response to a policy change is apt to be in the opposite direction from the long term effect. This is especially treacherous. A policy change which improves matters in the short run lays a foundation for degradation in the long run . . . short run versus long-run reversal processes are all around us . . . a student forgoes short-term earnings opportunities by attending college in order to increase his longer-term earning capability. This reversal between the short run and the long run occurs repeatedly.[1]

REALIZE INITIAL DIFFICULTY IN WRITING OBJECTIVES

Administrators, supervisors and teachers will undoubtedly experience trouble in writing objectives. This is to be expected; however, each subsequent school year, the staff should gain adequate proficiency in their development. The school with progress on its agenda permits each student to develop according to his own individual growth, talents, skills, etc. The objective-centered appraisal program permits each administrator, supervisor and teacher to develop his own skills according to his own talents, skills and pace. It may be necessary for one department to proceed and implement the program while another department is working on developing clearly defined objectives. This too is to be expected. No one department should keep another department from spurring ahead if adequate skills have been developed.

ANTICIPATE IMPROVEMENT IN COMMUNICATION NET-WORK

The objective-centered approach to performance appraisal should improve communications which must be a major concern to administrators. Communication is essential to and aided by the objective-

---

[1] Jay W. Forrester. "Systems Analysis As a Tool for Urban Planning," Mass. Institute of Tech., Cambridge, Mass., 1969, p. 15, (mimeographed paper).

centered approach to performance appraisal. Administrators cannot assume that teachers understand the purpose of or are aware of either their own goals or those of the school district. Rensis Likert states:

> Hostility, fear, distrust, and similar attitudes tend not only to reduce the flow and acceptance of relevant information, but also to evoke motives to distort communications both upward and downward. Distrust and lack of confidence leads members of an organization at all ends in the hierarchy to play it close to the chest, to share a minimum of information with others and to look with suspicion at the information passed on by others. Distrust leads to communication failures. Reciprocal confidence and trust on the part of the members of an organization seem necessary if the communication process is to function effectively.[2]

TEACH GOAL APPRECIATION

Explaining the objectives of the school district is only a partial fulfillment of an administrator's own communication and educational responsibilities toward his staff. The administrator must make certain that his staff appreciates the purpose of the school system. Each educator should know how his own performance and job contribute to the overall objectives. A planned and continuous program for effective communication is essential—for at no time does the school organization cease to have changes in all objectives. One of the major challenges of the school administrator is to develop a program of continuous goal appreciation by all staff members. To achieve this, the administrator must implement a process of studying, refining and reorienting all of the educators' thinking on the attainment of the objectives.

INTRODUCING THE OBJECTIVE-CENTERED PERFORMANCE APPRAISAL PROGRAM

The first stage in acquainting administrators with the objective-centered approach to performance appraisal should be designed to secure their understanding and commitment to the approach. The chances of doing this will be improved if a concentrated effort is

---

[2] Rensis Likert. *New Patterns of Management*, McGraw-Hill Book Company, Inc., New York, N.Y., 1961, p. 45.

made not to cram administrators with too much material and information all at one time.

The introduction of the programs will vary according to school district. Much will depend on such factors as commitment, training and experience of the administrator and the degree to which performance objectives have been used in the school district in the past. Some schools have used an on-the-job training approach in which administrators get relatively easy objectives and slowly progress to more challenging and meaningful objectives. In-service education courses have also been used to introduce the objective-centered performance appraisal program in a school system.

ON-THE-JOB TRAINING APPROACH

Through this approach the concept of objective-centered performance appraisal programs to school personnel becomes a continuous part of the everyday activities of the school system. The training program is integrated with the on-the-job "realities." Some educators have preferred this approach to the in-service approach because it is rather easy to administer and it gives quick results. It has been observed that an educator who has been trained to use this approach tends to be able to develop more clearly designed performance objectives.

• **Step I.** Conduct briefing sessions; concentrate on the following:

1. Explain performance objectives; how they are set. What are the advantages of using objectives?
2. Discuss the three components of a performance objective.
3. Demonstrate actual objectives which have been developed by the Board of Education and the chief school officer and show how progress against these objectives will be measured.
4. Have each administrator develop an objective for himself and discuss with the training group the weak and strong points of each developed objective.
5. Charge each administrator with the responsibility for preparing three long range goals and short range objectives and action plans for discussion at an objective discussion session, to be scheduled at a later date. These goals and objectives should be submitted prior to the session so that they may be evaluated and recommendations made.

6. Review each of the administrators' initial objectives within the next two weeks.
7. Give each administrator a bibliography of suggested readings on the subject of management by objectives.

• **Step II.** At this stage the chief school officer or the training administrator should schedule individual sessions with each administrator to review his individual objectives. This session is essentially a coaching session designed specifically for the purpose of counseling the individual administrator in setting his objectives and to sharpen up his Statement of Performance Objectives. This counseling session should work this way, as explained by Edward C. Schleh.

> The training administrator should first discuss the general conditions under which the administrator will be working and in a broad way point out to the administrator, the overall expectation in school objectives. In a way he is pointing out the general track on which the total operation is running. It is also helpful for the training administrator to point out some of the places in the administrator's job where he thinks objectives might be especially worthwhile that year. He should then ask the man to take this information, carefully review his own sphere of action, and come back later to suggest what he considers to be sound objectives for himself. The training administrator should exercise great care by avoiding stating objectives for the administrator. The administrator should develop on his own. The following are significant questions which should be answered in this session:

> 1. Are the objectives stated in specific observable terms?
> 2. Are the objectives relevant to the administrator's responsibilities?
> 3. Are the objectives realistic and challenging?
> 4. Are short range objectives related to the long range objectives?
> 5. Are standards necessary for certain objectives?
> 6. Are action plans sequential, specific and stated with target dates?
> 7. Do the objectives meet the criteria as stated in Chapter Four?

   8 . Are the long range objectives compatible with the philosophy and educational goals of the school district? [3]

The training administrator and the administrator should agree upon target dates for the achievement of each objective. The next step involves mutually agreeing on objectives and recording them in writing in a Statement of Performance Objectives. One copy is kept by the administrator and one copy is kept by the training administrator.

. Step III. This step should take place ten weeks after the beginning of school. However, some schools may wish to increase this time period by a few weeks, particularly if the program is being implemented for the first time. This step will involve review and critique of an administrator's performance. Similar to Step II, the training administrator's attitude should be that of an understanding coach and the entire conference should be conducted on an individual basis.

At this time it is extremely important that each and every objective which was mutually agreed upon be reviewed. In this and subsequent conference sessions on performance appraisal the administrator should understand that his performance will be evaluated against the objectives which he has set for himself in the Statement of Performance Objectives.

Chapter Nine discusses performance review in detail. Briefly, the performance review conference should be used to:

1 . Assess the administrator's progress according to the Statement of Performance Objectives.
2 . Evaluate the validity of the initial objectives.
3 . Make necessary modifications, revisions and deletions in the objectives and action plans.
4 . Add new short range objectives in order to progress and reach the long range goals.
5 . Make necessary changes in writing.

The performance review conference should begin with the training administrator providing the administrator with assistance for reaching the objectives and appraising success in his objectives. This appraisal

---

[3] Edward C. Schleh, *Management by Results*. McGraw-Hill Book Company, Inc., New York, N.Y., 1961, p. 38.

should be based on the objective-centered approach. It should never include the trait approach.

• Step IV. After Steps I, II and III have been completed, Step IV involves getting the rest of the staff involved in the program. The approach used should be similar to those cited above for administrators.

IN-SERVICE EDUCATION APPROACH

Through this approach, formal courses of instruction are presented by educators within the school district and/or educators employed in other schools, colleges, universities or educational agencies. This approach usually replicates the kind of training usually offered in higher educational institutions.

The following is a list of three avenues for implementing this in-service course.

1. The in-service course can be conducted by a private consultant firm. If the school district chooses this method, the consultant firm should be retained from the inception of the program to the end. This helps to insure continuity and makes for a smoothly operating program. Consultants can usually be obtained by contacting local colleges and universities. Schools such as Harvard, M.I.T. and the University of Michigan can be helpful in recommending outstanding people in this area.

2. A school district may prefer to run the in-service course themselves, using their own administrators, supervisors and teachers assisted by outside consultants. Schools that have used this method have found that in some cases the consultants were needed more than have been anticipated.

3. The American Management Association periodically runs a number of workshops and management institutes which could prove valuable to school districts contemplating implementing the objective-centered approach to performance appraisal. This organization may be able to recommend outstanding business consultants who are able to relate management by objectives to education. Administrators should consider benefits to be derived from this source very carefully. Many of the problems which have perplexed business management have been solved by time and experience; to the extent that school districts resemble business enterprise much can be learned this way.

THE FORMAT FOR THE IN-SERVICE EDUCATION

The first stage for conducting the in-service course or workshop should be to introduce and acquaint administrators, supervisors and teachers with the system of school management by objectives and explain how it is related to the objective-centered appraisal program so that they may gain an understanding and acceptance of the program. A dynamic consultant can introduce the concept to the staff in an attractive and appealing manner. One school district hired a number of teachers who had had experience with school management by objectives to appear at the first in-service course to share their experiences with the staff.

A. The first in-service course should also include an explanation of the new administrative policy and procedure for implementing the objective-centered performance appraisal program.

B. This helps to give the administrator and teachers an idea of how extensively the program will be implemented. The administrative policy and procedural guidelines are developed to avoid any misunderstanding and to reduce conflicts.

METHODS AND TECHNIQUES FOR INSTRUCTING THE IN-SERVICE COURSE

A variety of methods and techniques can be employed in the in-service course in order to meet differences in staff preferences.

The following methods have been found to be effective:

A. Sound Film Strip Presentation

A sound film strip on school management by objectives should prove helpful in introducing the system to the participants. There are a number of film strips on behavioral objectives which could also prove valuable in aiding the staff in writing objectives.

B. Workbooks

Workbooks commercially developed or written by the in-service course leader should prove extremely helpful as the basic source for training personnel in the system. There are a number of workbooks developed on behavioral objectives which can also aid the staff in developing their own objectives.

C. Role Playing

Role playing is an effective technique to simulate a real-life situation. This technique is effective in demonstrating how the negotiation session and the interview conference between the administrator and the teacher should be conducted to review objectives and evaluate performance.

D. Medium and Large Group Lectures

These grouping patterns should be helpful in explaining the structural framework of school management by objectives and various other aspects of the program.

E. Small Group Presentation

This grouping pattern has been helpful in criticizing goal and objective statements and to provide additional training for those needing it. It is also recommended that during small group discussions time should be given to "meshing" individual objectives with those of the department, building and school district.

An administrative policy and procedural statement on school management by objectives should be worked out in advance by the chief school officer and assisted by someone thoroughly familiar with the concept. This statement places substance behind the program.

In essence, these operational procedures act as a basic guide for demonstrating the following:

- Who in the area, department, school building or school district is responsible for initiating objective setting.
- To whom the proposed objectives will be directed for review, amendments and mutual agreement.
- Who is responsible for administering the appraisal performance review.
- Who will reconcile disagreement over objectives.

The operational procedure for developing objectives is an extension of line of authority chart. The appendix at the rear of this book illustrates such a policy and procedural statement for implementing an objective-centered performance appraisal program.

The course content for the in-service program for implementing the objective-centered performance appraisal approach is illustrated in Figure 2-1 and is described below.

Session No. 1—Guiding and Directing for Setting Objectives

These sessions should deal with counseling the educator for setting objectives. Specifically these sessions should concentrate on the following:

1. What are the procedures for guiding and directing the educator for setting objectives?
2. What is the function of job description in setting objectives?
3. How should the strengths and weaknesses in areas by responsibilities be assessed?
4. How should the educator be placed on track for achieving objectives?
5. What activities should be discussed during the guidance and directing conference?

Session No. 2—Setting Objectives

There should be several sessions under this course outlined. Here are the main questions which should be answered in these sessions:

1. What are performance objectives?
2. What is the differentiation between long range goals and short range objectives?
3. What are the three components of objectives?
4. What are characteristics of well-written objectives?
5. What are long and short range objectives and what is their interrelationship?
6. What are standards, constraints, and action plans?
7. How are performance objectives recorded?
8. What is meant by mutually agreeing on objectives?

Session No. 3—Achieving Objectives

This session should deal primarily with how an educator should proceed to achieve his objectives. At this session, the following should be included:

1. How should effective use be made of the action plans?
2. How should problems associated with objective attainment be analyzed and recorded?
3. What is the rationale for self-evaluating performance?

Session No. 4—Conducting the Post-Appraisal Conference

These sessions are extremely important because unless they are carried out successfully, the effectiveness of the appraisal program will be greatly reduced. These sessions should deal with the following important items:

1. How is the comparison made between actual results and anticipated results?
2. What appropriate actions should be taken to correct performance?
3. How should objectives and action plans be modified and revised?
4. What is meant by coaching and counseling?
5. What is a directed conference? A non-directed conference?
6. What are effective conference techniques?
7. What should be the frequency for assessing performance?
8. What is the difference between the "trait" and "result" performance appraisal approaches?
9. How should performance outcome be recorded on the Performance Appraisal Review form?

Every effort must be made to convince administrators who will be administering the performance appraisal program that it will be an aid to them not only in improving their own individual performance, but also the performance of their staff members, which will eventually lead to improving student performance.

SUMMARY

Some requisites for the effective implementation of an objective-centered performance appraisal program are: obtain commitment from the top; keep paperwork and clerical chores to a minimum; consider a modest beginning; communicate to the staff.

There are two approaches for introducing the objective-centered performance appraisal program in school districts:

1. On-the-job training. Through this approach, introducing the program to school personnel becomes a continuous part of every day activities.

2. In-service education course. Through this approach, formal courses of instruction are presented by educators within or out of the school district.

THREE

Defining the Structure for Setting Objectives

There can be no real basis for planning day-to-day school activities without the establishment and identification of objectives towards which the professional talents of the educators are to be directed. Objectives may be stated in terms of academic achievement scores, test results, standards, target dates, budget reduction, quotas, purposes—in fact, there is an endless variety. All objectives must identify with an established goal toward which the school district wishes to exert motion by marshalling the necessary talents and resources to reach it. However, regardless of the terms used, objectives must be understandable and must permit the actual measurement of minimal acceptable performance. Objectives must be stated in specific terms, figures or standards that are meaningful to the administrators and teachers whose progress and results are to be appraised.

The purposes of this chapter are to more fully state the rationale of management by objectives, to define school management by objectives, to explain the essential factors of a performance objective, to focus on making objectives future oriented; to describe line-staff relationship in setting objectives, to identify the procedural steps for setting objectives, to explain multiple level objectives and to move from setting objectives to attaining objectives.

THE RATIONALE FOR OBJECTIVES

John F. Mee of Indiana University has stated that in order to develop a philosophy for operating an organization that will be effectively carried out, a combination of objectives will be required.[1]

This statement is predicated on the idea that unless specific objectives are set, agreed to and performed on all levels of operating the school system, there will be relatively little basis for measuring the effectiveness of administrators or teachers. The significant point here is that the predetermination of desired objectives has resulted in the formulation of the rationale for objectives. The rationale may be stated as follows: Before the school system can be operated efficiently, there must be specific levels of objectives and they must be exactly determined, understood and recorded. When these objectives have been developed, Mee goes on to say that administrators have the essential functions for:

1. Planning to achieve the predetermined multi-level objective.
2. Organizing to put the plans into action.
3. Motivating the teachers to execute the plan.
4. Monitoring the activities in conformance to the plan.

The most desired manner for the administrator to execute his professional function is through the process known as school management by objectives.

SCHOOL MANAGEMENT BY OBJECTIVES

School management by objectives describes the administrative process whereby all efforts of the school system are organized in terms of achieving specific results by an established time. Implicit in the process is the requirement that the specific results contribute to achieving the clearly stated long range objectives of the school organization.

School management by objectives emphasizes the goals to be achieved. Everything—educational goals, plans, policies, organizational structure, and the responsibilities of individual educators—is related to and determined by the goals and objectives.

In a school system which has implemented school management by objectives, realistic and challenging goals are set and teachers and administrators are expected to achieve their objectives. These objectives are set neither so low that poor performance can go by nor so high

[1] John F. Mee, "Management Philosophy for Professional Executives," *Business Horizons*, Supplement to the *Indiana Business Review*, February, 1957, p. 5.

that one has to be a superman to achieve them. The objectives are the results that can reasonably be expected if an educator works diligently to fulfill his professional responsibility.

Objectives are designed to get results. Thus, a suitable objective would not be "reducing teachers' absentee rate." Even "conducting studies of the causes of student drop-out and how it might be reduced" would not be accepted as specific and result-oriented enough. Instead, a suitable objective might be "to reduce teacher absentee rate by 50% within one year."

It is of course recognized that all results cannot be stated quantitatively. However, even in areas where short-term results are hard to quantify, the results that are expected can be improved. For example, "to maintain an adequate appraisal program," might be improved "to complete appraisal on all professional positions by December 15."

DEFINING A PERFORMANCE OBJECTIVE

Before going any further in this chapter, it is appropriate to define performance objective.

Although there are perhaps a hundred variations in the definition of a performance objective, the author feels satisfied with the following definition:

A performance objective is a statement of a personal commitment to a specific accomplishment or result that is:

- Oriented towards fulfilling the mission of the school system;
- Stated in observable terms;
- Valuable for achieving the purpose of the school system;
- Worthwhile for improving performance;
- Beneficial in monitoring performance;
- Time-phased for achieving results.

OBJECTIVE SETTING MUST BE FUTURE ORIENTED

Normally teachers are inclined to set objectives only in relation to their own team, department or areas of responsibility. This is bound to occur if they are not familiar with the school district's organizational objectives. An acute problem which has been observed by the author is that when teachers were asked to participate in the objective setting process, they had a tendency to set low risk bearing objectives in order not to make them too difficult to achieve. If this tencency goes unchecked, the appraisal program is heading for disaster. Low risk bearing objectives generate low satisfaction among the professional staff and efforts must be taken to correct this situation immediately.

The process of setting objectives determines to a large extent how fast the school district will improve. In too many school districts setting objectives simply means reviewing last year's appraisal forms and then setting comparable objectives for the ensuing school year. This type of procedure completely ignores the possibility that last year's objectives may have been all right at that time, but changing times bring on changing conditions. Setting objectives must not focus too much on the past. It must take the present conditions into consideration and it must be future oriented. All efforts must be united towards the common goal of maximizing the total talents of the available resources in order to set and achieve objectives.

LINE-STAFF RELATIONSHIP IN SETTING OBJECTIVES

In the traditional school organization, the authority, responsibility and accountability for the operation of the school district are lodged in the chief school officer. He delegates some of his authority and responsibility to members of his central administration staff and holds them accountable for the achievement of specific objectives. They, in turn, delegate part of their authority and responsibility, and so on. The delegation of authority and responsibility proceeds down through the school organization. In the traditional school organization set-up all authority or influence seems to be coming from the top and is generated downward.

However, when the objective-centered approach to performance appraisal is established in a school district, the authority or influence is generated *downward, upward* and *sideward*.[2] Therefore, the different levels of the school organization should not be thought of as different

---

[2] Rensis Likert, *New Patterns of Management*. McGraw-Hill Book Co., New York, N.Y., 1961, pp. 97-118.

levels of authority but rather as coordinating or linking larger or smaller numbers of performing groups. At the top and central level of the school organization, the strengths, weaknesses, objectives, recommendations, and influence processes of a larger number of school units or departments would converge because of Rensis Likert's linking pin concept or overlapping group structure which emanates for resolving conflicts and integrating decisions. The top level of the school organization coordinates decisions which affect and influence a greater number of administrators, supervisors and teachers. This does not necessarily mean that the chief school officer would always exert more influence on performance. This may mean however, that a teacher in the classroom may exert more influence on an important decision affecting the school system than the superintendent.

The traditional concept in school organization that line has authority and staff is advisory has gradually been breaking down in education, even though administrators in education seem to be looking the other way. When the objective-centered approach to appraisal is implemented, the problems associated with line-staff relationships tend to be mitigated in an atmosphere of setting objectives, interacting and mutually agreeing on them, thus providing an effective motivating climate by coaching and counseling. The interaction that characterizes the objective-centered approach provides the mechanism that enables a school organization to arrive at sound decisions through an integrated approach to improving the effectiveness of the school system. Line and staff contributions to achieving objectives will vary with each objective and with the available resources which each possessed. When line and staff relationship is improved in this manner, line does not have the sole responsibility and authority to make decisions with staff looking over line's shoulders. Line does, however, have the authority and responsibility for creating an improved working environment through an objective-centered approach through which objectives are set and mutually agreed to. Thus, both line and staff contribute to the much improved school complex.

The linking pin concept may appear to be merely a restatement of the function of school organization of any school system. However, the main difference under the linking pin concept lies in the administrator's perception of his own job or function and his behavior growing out of his perception. In Likert's theory the administrator becomes a linking pin in that he not only assumes a role of a connector of two groups, he is also a member of two groups:

1. He is a member of his peers. All building principals who may be identified as middle management report to the assistant superintendent or superintendent.
2. He is also a member of a group which he may be in charge of, not as a superior, but as a supportive member of a department, etc.

In this context, the linking pin concept stresses the importance of administrators interacting effectively with their individual groups. Effective group interaction is seen here as open communication within the group, development of mutual trust, mutual agreement on decision making, group objective setting, and the definition of roles and shared responsibility. The results of effective group interaction will produce group accountability, group loyalty, improved cohesiveness and individual responsibility with the objective of the group. In essence, for an administrator to become a real linking pin, there must be real interaction between himself and the members of his group.[3]

IDENTIFYING THE PROCEDURAL STEPS FOR SETTING OBJECTIVES

At this point, the reader should be ready to examine the process by which objectives are set for all levels within the school system beginning at the very top with the board of education and gradually working down to the level the school wishes to cover. The sequential

---

[3] *Comment from the Author*: Recently, a prominent behavioral theorist, was very critical of the way one particular school system had blamed the destruction between line and staff relationship because the system had developed equivocal line of authority and responsibility. To some administrators this may mean that staff personnel are more useful when they serve as consultants to line personnel with no local authority than outside consultants. The intent of this organizational pattern is based upon the premise that when staff serves as consultants rather than supervisors, they have responsibilities for completing specific objectives, such as conducting in-service programs, accounting for school funds, researching problems, etc. Line personnel are responsible for managing the operations of teachers, negotiating objectives, etc. This may be true in some school systems; however, this author has found the opposite to be true, that is, when certain staff members are given specific authority and responsibility, the system tends to operate efficiently. Take for example the director of curriculum and instruction who has supervisory responsibility. The director not only serves as a consultant, but also has responsibility in negotiating objectives with building principals on all matters pertaining to curriculum and instruction and assumes responsibility and accountability for the entire instructional program. Therefore, the person employed as an "expert" in curriculum and instruction has direct authority to influence a greater number of persons. The author does suggest, however, that each school system should adopt an organizational pattern, which best meets the need of that system.

steps for setting objectives should proceed in definite steps as illustrated in Figure 3-1 and in the indicated order as summarized below:

1. Initiating Needs Assessment Study.
2. Setting Long-Range Goals.
3. Conducting Briefing Sessions on Setting Objectives.
4. Setting Line Objectives.
5. Setting Staff Objectives.
6. Reporting Results.

INITIATING NEEDS ASSESSMENT STUDY

The first step in setting objectives is to organize a Special Task Force Council composed of parents, teachers, students, school administrators, school board members, concerned citizens—representing every social, economic, racial and ethnic group of the community, to analyze the problems or needs of the school district. Needs can be identified as deviations or differences between what exists and what is desired—which represents a gap in performance of the school district. Once these differences are determined, solutions through the fulfillment of performance objectives can be developed for closing the gap.

By analyzing the needs in this manner, additional students' needs may be discovered which most likely will necessitate revisions in the present philosophy and educational goals of the school district.

The following questions must be considered in order to adequately revise the present philosophy and educational goals of the school district:

- What are the purposes of the school district?
- Do the present educational goals specify the school district's philosophy in terms of students' achievement, attitude and behavior?
- Which educational goals should have priority?
- Do parents, teachers, and students understand and accept the educational goals of the school district?
- Is the school district making progress toward meeting its educational goals?
- How does the school district identify the changes occurring in the local, state, national and world-wide community? How does the school district prepare its students to react with understanding to changes occurring presently and in the future?

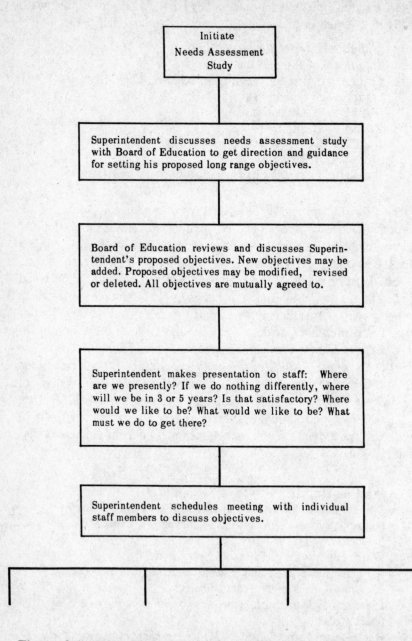

Figure 3-1 THE SEQUENTIAL STEPS FOR SETTING OB-
JECTIVES

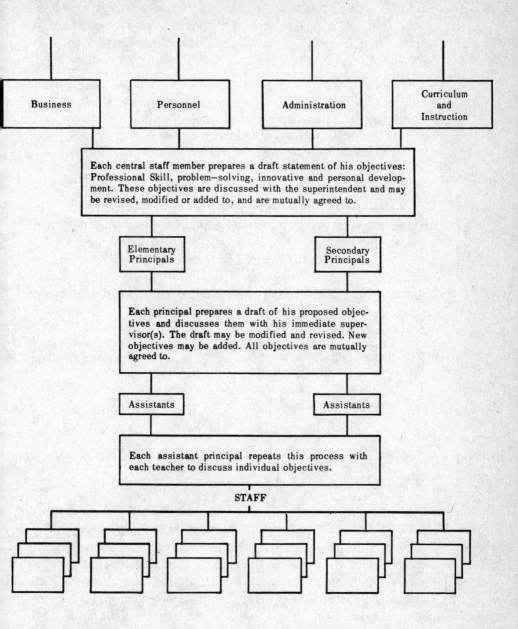

| Business | Personnel | Administration | Curriculum and Instruction |

Each central staff member prepares a draft statement of his objectives: Professional Skill, problem—solving, innovative and personal development. These objectives are discussed with the superintendent and may be revised, modified or added to, and are mutually agreed to.

| Elementary Principals | | Secondary Principals |

Each principal prepares a draft of his proposed objectives and discusses them with his immediate supervisor(s). The draft may be modified and revised. New objectives may be added. All objectives are mutually agreed to.

| Assistants | | Assistants |

Each assistant principal repeats this process with each teacher to discuss individual objectives.

STAFF

Once the philosophy and educational goals have been thoroughly discussed, analyzed and recorded, the next important step in initiating the Needs Assessment Study is to study the various areas of the school district, but, before we proceed with this step, it is appropriate at this time to define a Needs Assessment Study. New Jersey State Department of Education has published the following definition:

> A needs assessment study is an activity by which the school personnel, students and community members appraise the effectiveness of the school systems in terms of existing philosophy and education, goals, strengths and weaknesses. From this study, educational goals, long-range objectives, short-range objectives, and action plans are developed to correct the weaknesses of the school system.[4]

The Needs Assessment Study should consider: (1) strengths of the existing program—what are we doing to develop our philosophy and purposes? (2) weaknesses of the existing program; (3) plans for the future—how do we plan to overcome our weaknesses to meet our needs?

Each of these three aspects of the Needs Assessment Study should be examined as they relate to the following broad general areas of the school system:

1. Administration
2. Supervision and Counseling
3. Instruction
4. Instructional Materials
5. Pupil Personnel
6. Co-Curricular Program
7. Health and Nutrition
8. Community Relations
9. School Plant, Site and Equipment

Although the Special Task Force Council is charged with the responsibility for finalizing the Needs Assessment Study, it is customary for the council to organize a central planning committee composed of the chairman of the nine areas cited above. The central planning committee should facilitate the collection, study and analysis of the data collected for the nine areas. The information is then discussed and interpreted to the Special Task Force Council so that a valid assessment is brought about through the concentrated efforts of both groups.

---

[4] New Jersey State Department of Education, "District-Wide Improvement Program." Trenton, N. J. p. 3, (pamphlet).

All of the efforts which have been directed to gather pertinent information about student's learning and the learning environment should lead to the finalization of the study. The final step of the study should evidence identifying priorities. These priorities then become the basis for setting long range goals and short range objectives.

The author will not attempt to elaborate any further on initiating Needs Assessment Study. To provide adequate coverage of this subject would require a book. However, additional information can be obtained by delving into the literature mentioned in the bibliography.

SETTING LONG-RANGE GOALS

Once the Needs Assessment Study has been completed, a copy of the study is forwarded to each board member for review. At a special meeting of the board, the superintendent, assisted by the Special Task Force Council should discuss in detail the various strengths and weaknesses of the nine areas stated in the Needs Assessment Study. Using this information, the board of education designates priority areas and directs and guides the chief school officer in drafting long-range goals[5] for the school system. Armed with this information, the top school executive officer meets with his central administration staff, discusses the priority areas, and listens to their suggestions and recommendations for finalizing the long-range goals.

A copy of the long range goals is presented to each member for review prior to a meeting for goal setting. At a special meeting called by the president of the board, each goal is scrutinized and revised if necessary. Additional goals may originate from the meeting. When all of the goals have been reviewed and changes denoted, the long range goals are voted on as a package and approved by the board of education. Some board members may say that these are the superintendent's goals, not the board's. The chief school officer is a member of the board. Although he has no voting power, he acts in their behalf. David E. Olsson has something to say on this matter:

> . . . the board usually reserves to itself the responsibility and authority for deciding on long range objectives, policies proposed and budgets . . . When the board fails to set realistic challenges,

---

[5] Long range goals are discussed in Chapter Four.

long range objectives, it fails to perform one of its primary roles—that of providing guidance and evaluation.[6]

After the long range goals have been approved by the board, the superintendent prepares to disseminate these goals to the staff in written form and by making a presentation before the entire staff.

CONDUCTING BRIEFING SESSIONS ON SETTING OBJECTIVES

Assisted by the central administrative staff, the chief school officer prepares a speech to introduce the concept of school management by objectives and the objective-centered approach to performance appraisal to the entire staff of the school system. The briefing session should be held on the first day of school in a large auditorium. While it is preferable to address the entire school staff at one time, in some large districts it may be necessary to use closed circuit television or video tape to reach everyone. The superintendent's presentation should answer the following questions:

- What is the present condition of the school system? What services do we offer to our students? What kind of services do our parents want from us?
- What techniques do we use to monitor performance of teachers? Of students? What experimental projects are implemented in the district to improve the school's effectiveness?
- Who are our students? What changes have come about in the local community, state, country and the world which will have a direct influence and impact on the school system?
- If we did nothing different from our present methods and teachings, where would the school system be in three years? In five years?
- Is this outcome sufficient for us? What are some goals we would like to see advanced in the school system?
- Given ideal objectives, what could each administrator, teacher and other employee of the school system do differently or stop doing in order to move the entire school organization for-

---

[6] David E. Olsson, *Management by Objectives*. Pacific Books Publishers, Palo Alto, California, 1968, p. 88.

ward? In teaching? In human relations? In school management development?

When the superintendent completes this part of his presentation, he should announce the long range goals which have been approved by the board of education and issue a written copy to each staff member.

The next phase is to set line objectives.

SETTING LINE OBJECTIVES

The chief school officer determines those of his central administrative staff with whom he will personally review objectives. In a large school district, he may wish to see only those of his immediate staff, such as the deputy, associate and assistant superintendent. In a small school district, he may wish to review the objectives of all administrators and supervisors.

Objective setting certainly cannot be limited to administrators. Each administrator must use the same objective setting technique with each supervisor, teacher and supportive personnel.

Each administrator must communicate his individual goals to the staff; the staff members will then go through the same procedural steps, taking the objectives of their supervisors as a base, translating them into a plan of action, and finally presenting their own proposed objectives. Each staff member will usually select goals which are pertinent to his own area of responsibility which is necessarily narrow in scope.

The reason for setting line objectives first becomes apparent when one understands the nature and scope of line responsibility. Line is generally responsible for carrying out the "mission" of the school system. Thus, if the board of education sets a long-range goal, "to increase the number of students on grade level in math . . . ," all of the efforts of line personnel will be exerted in that direction. The math objective will be set first by the building principals so that the personnel in each of the schools will set and synchronize individual goals with those of the school district. It would be foolish for teachers to set objectives without first knowing what goals were set by the board of education and the school officers, or for that matter, the building principal.

Each line personnel is responsible for a segment of the school system's overall activity and, therefore, should make certain that the following guidelines are adhered to in their particular area:

1. All administrators should set long range goals and short-range objectives.
2. Individual school objectives and area objectives should be coordinated with the school system's long-range goals.
3. Objectives should include sub-objectives in terms of an action plan and check points for monitoring performance.
4. Objectives should not only encompass the traditional accomplishments of the school system; but also provide for growth and achievement.

Each line personnel who is responsible for a segment of the overall objectives of the school system must accept the responsibilities for achieving his own results as well as those of his staff. The line personnel must also be concerned that the school system achieves the long-range goals set by the board of education.

SETTING STAFF OBJECTIVES

Once long-range goals and line objectives have been developed, it then becomes necessary for the formulation of staff objectives. By setting objectives in this fashion, unnecessary staff activities are avoided because only those staff activities which are necessary to achieve long range goals and line objectives will be undertaken.

In a situation whereby the superintendent is aiming to reduce teacher absentee rate, the principals and individual teachers must have as one of their objectives a plan which will help reduce the teacher absentee rate. In a situation in which the director of curriculum and instruction aims at increasing the number of students reading on grade level, the elementary principal and teachers must have as one of their objectives the necessary reading program that will help produce the required results. Thus, it should become clear to the reader why long range goals and line objectives must be set first and then staff objectives.

REPORTING ON RESULTS

The chief school officer is responsible for the culminating phase of the first school year (and each year thereafter) of operating the school under a system of school management by objectives. He should call a meeting of the entire staff for the purpose of having each administrator report on the results achieved. Each building principal and member of the central administration staff uses the following agenda to report results to the staff.

1. State objectives which were set and mutually agreed to by the teachers and administrators.
2. Explain those objectives which were successfully achieved.
3. Explain the differences between results achieved and anticipated results and the reasons for the differences.
4. State the objectives set for the next school year with dates for quarterly review of performance.

One should not underestimate the powerful effect of peer opinion and influence on goal setting and achievement. One effective way to stimulate teachers and administrators and other employees to change their direction, behavior and attitude for improved performance is for their immediate supervisor to promise to achieve certain stated objectives before an audience of community members (some of whom are employees of the school system) and other staff members.

The superintendent should terminate the meeting by making some general comments about the school district's overall performance in regard to achieving objectives, commenting on the new objectives which were set and wishing the entire staff a well-deserved, enjoyable vacation.

MOVING FROM SETTING OBJECTIVES TO
ATTAINING OBJECTIVES

The benefits to be derived from setting objectives lies not only in the process of establishing objectives, but in the activities that follow to insure achievement. Very little is accomplished if objectives are set by line personnel but not transmitted to the staff personnel primarily responsible for making them a reality. The following guides should prove helpful when goal oriented personnel move from setting objectives to attaining objectives:

- Objectives should be clearly stated, in writing.

- Objectives which require supporting information should be accurately and fully explained to each employee who has a responsibility for achieving them.

- All administrators and teachers of the school district should understand how they and their area of responsibility fit into the total objectives of the school system.

- Each educator should be able to determine how his personal goals can be satisfied through the achievement of the school organizational goals.

- Motivation must be applied and maintained at all times to ensure that maximum effort is being exerted to achieve the school system's gains.

- Administration's concern must be given to timing, logistics, flexible, adequate checkpoints, and the adjustment of the action plan in pursuit of the ultimate objectives.

- Educational goals should be broken down into sub-goals and sub-sub-goals until they have meaning to all personnel.

- Allowances must be made for revising, modifying or even discarding goals if circumstances change after the goal has been set.

- Comprehensive plans must be set in motion and must be redefined and modified until the school system's goal and the personal goals of each educator have reached an effective balance.[7]

EXPLAINING MULTIPLE LEVEL OBJECTIVES

The maximum benefits derived from school management by objectives are achieved by applying the concept at all levels of the school system—effectiveness is likely to increase with number. To illustrate,

---

[7] Ray A. Killian, *Managing by Design for Maximum Executive Effectiveness*, American Management Association, Inc., New York, N.Y., 1968, p. 77. The author has paraphrased and related to education the original text of Ray A. Killian.

a long range goal has been set by the board of education to increase the number of students reading on grade level. The director of curriculum, director of personnel, the elementary reading supervisors, the individual building principals, the assistant principals, the library media specialists, the team leaders and the teachers must establish compatible objectives at their respective levels for meeting the long range goals of the board of education.

Similarly, if the director of pupil personnel is required to increase the number of students scoring 1000 or more on the Scholastic Aptitude Test from 10% to 50%, a number of educators—the director of guidance, the principal, the assistant principal and the teachers—must exert efforts for achieving a stated portion of the director's objectives.

As soon as line and staff objectives have been established on the basis of and consistent with the long range goals of the board of education, and as soon as their objectives have been translated into action plans at each level within each school department and team, the school system has a complete charter of what is necessary in order to achieve long range goals of the board for the ensuing school year.

A total school system plan has been developed, and each school employee is aware of what must be accomplished to achieve his objectives. The long range school goals have been broken down into objectives for multiple levels of school management and in a controllable manner.

SUMMARY

The philosophy behind objectives is that unless specific objectives on all levels of operating the school system are set, mutually agreed to and performed, there will be relatively little value or basis for measuring the performance of educators. School management by objectives is the process by which all the efforts of the employees of a school system are exerted toward achieving specific objectives within established time periods. A statement of objective is a personal commitment to a specific act or results. Objective setting must be future oriented. When the objective-centered approach to performance appraisal is established in a school district, the authority influence for performance is generated forward, upward, and sideward. The procedural steps for setting objectives are: (1) Initiating Needs Assessment Study; (2) Setting Long-Range Goals; (3) Conducting Briefing Session on Setting Objectives; (4) Setting Line Objectives; (5) Setting Staff Objectives; (6) Reporting on Results.

Maximum benefits can be derived from school management by objectives when the process has been applied to all levels of the school system. The benefit to be derived from setting objectives lies not only in the process of setting objectives but in the follow-up activities and the implementation of objectives.

FOUR

Writing Well-Defined Performance Objectives

The writing of well-defined performance objectives is perhaps the most important activity to be completed by each school person involved in performance appraisal. Without objectives, an act or activity has very little meaning. A person who is contemplating taking a trip would not do so without first referring to a map to guide him to his destination. Neither administrators nor teachers should perform in a school system without *written* statements of clearly defined performance objectives.

Most public school systems cannot afford to operate on a "trial and error" basis. Performance objectives guide the selection of activities for reaching a goal. Special circumstances or conditions may be recognized and success criteria stated in order to evaluate performance. Therefore, the setting and development of well-defined objectives is an important aspect of an effective performance appraisal and development program.

This chapter will discuss the value of writing performance objectives, enumerate the guidelines for developing performance objectives, explain the characteristics of well-defined objectives, state how to write minimal standards to measure the unmeasurable, provide guidance for developing objectives in observable terms, delineate how to write action plans for objectives, and describe two major classifications of objectives.

VALUE OF WRITING PERFORMANCE OBJECTIVES

At the present time, the administration, supervision and teaching in the public schools is such that many school districts operate more or less on an unclear basis. Although objectives are identified, they usually are stated in broad, general terms which permit school personnel to wander or stray from their individual assignments which also are not explicitly defined. Time often is not used efficiently, individual tasks are not achieved, and school personnel are ineffectively evaluated. The result is poor performance on the part of students as well as school personnel. Performance objectives in the professional appraisal and development program have some specific values which need to be delineated:

1. They provide a clear focus for performance activity and in so doing help all school personnel to develop or choose more efficacious strategies for obtaining results.
2. They provide a means by which the school enters into a written agreement for performance.
3. They induce the administrators and teachers to make decisions which lead to successful performance.
4. Well-defined performance objectives provide for more efficient and effective use of time and effort.
5. They provide a means by which school personnel are able to periodically assess performance, therefore enabling continuous constructive changes in performance.
6. Unless performance objectives are clearly understood by administrators and teachers, evaluation of school personnel may be unfair.
7. When there are clearly stated long range goals and short range performance objectives, the educational system is able to judge personnel and district effectiveness.
8. They improve the professional training and development program by concentrating on skills, etc., needed to achieve definite goals.
9. They can be used as the basis for motivating educators to perform at a superior or improved level.
10. They tend to improve administrator-teacher relationship because they define task and responsibility.

The value of goals and objectives in a professional personnel appraisal program cannot be over-emphasized. The success or failure of a school system rests with the integration of clearly defined written performance objectives performed by a cadre of school personnel aiming to maximize the total effectiveness of the system for youngsters.

GUIDELINES FOR WRITING PERFORMANCE OBJECTIVES

The following rules will aid in the development of performance objectives. Although all objectives may not necessarily follow all of these guidelines, it is wise to check them out against each guide:

Performance objectives should specify a condition under which the act will be performed.

There are times when circumstances and conditions must be met if the objectives are to be achieved. For example, it may be necessary to specify constraining variables such as people, time, money, or certain equipment and materials. Such a portion of a performance objective is stated:

> Assisted by the Federal Aid Coordinator . . .

Performance objectives should specify in observable terms the specific act to be accomplished.

Accomplishment should emanate from some action. The commitment to this action is the basis upon which objectives are developed. The statement describing the act should use action verbs which can be evaluated in observable terms. Such a portion of a performance objective is stated:

> . . . to develop a retrieval system whereby guidance information on children who have moved out of Wyandanch School District . . .

Performance objectives should specify a standard of acceptable performance.

In order to determine whether or not a specific objective has been successfully achieved, it is necessary for some set of conditions to be identified describing what constitutes successful performance.

> . . . at least eighty per cent of my class will score on grade level using Series B of the Metropolitan Achievement Test in Reading no later than April 30, 1972.

Performance objectives should delineate single or key acts or performances.

If performance objectives are to be measured effectively, there must be clear evidence as to whether or not the objective has been achieved. Therefore, in order to avoid confusion, the objective should consider the performance of a single act. Multiple acts should be broken down according to individual objectives.

Performance objectives should state a projected date for accomplishment.

All performance objectives should include a date of completion. All professional skill objectives are implied to be completed within a period of one school year. An innovative objective should have a specific calendar date so that it can be determined whether or not the objective has been accomplished. Personal development objectives are usually specified for completion during the school year.

Performance objectives should relate to the individual role and authority and the overall objectives of the area, department and school system.

The achievement of objectives other than those directly related to one's responsibility is to be avoided at all costs. Side-tracking is common in almost every job. It comes about for many reasons—personal interest of an educator, lack of availability of a colleague, pet project of an administrator, traditional activities, to mention a few.

Performance objectives should be consistent with the school's philosophy and broad objectives.

Any objectives which conflict with board of education policies and procedures are to be avoided unless efforts are made to change the policy and procedure. Agreements with the teachers' organizations, ethical considerations and community relations must be considered.

Performance objectives must understandably be written by those who are responsible for achieving them.

As long as the objective is clear and understandable by those who are responsible for achievement, then the understanding by others is less important.

Performance objectives should be mutually agreed upon by both administrator and teacher.

Pressure or coercion, implied or otherwise, should not be used to get educators to agree to objectives. It would be ridiculous for an administrator to hand a teacher a statement of performance objectives and say, "These are your objectives." It is equally ridiculous for the teacher to say, "These are all the objectives I am going to work for." Performance objectives are statements of conditions to be achieved within a stated period of time. These objectives have been agreed upon, analyzed and identified. Of course, the administrator should influence the setting of objectives. This does not say that the objective cannot be negotiated by the administrators and teachers. In fact, negotiation is an important part of school management by objectives. The fact that either party may be guilty of setting unrealistic or unreachable objectives makes negotiation of objectives mandatory.

Performance objectives should be stated in writing; the signature of all parties concerned should be affixed to each copy and should be referred to periodically by all parties.

Human beings have a tendency to remember things that turn out well. They also have a tendency either to modify or forget those things which are undesirable. By stating objectives in writing this tendency is counteracted.

Performance objectives should not only be stated in writing but should also be discussed between all parties directly concerned.

Administrators should not forget that the success of their departments rests with how well the teachers perform their individual tasks. By discussing objectives face to face, opportunities are provided for an interchange of ideas when suggestions and recommendations can emanate not only from the administrators, but from the teachers as well. Dialogue is one of the most effective ways to build and maintain a congenial relationship among school personnel. Discussion also helps to clear up any misunderstandings about the achievement of any one objective.

Performance objectives should be realistic, attainable and represent a challenge.

All objectives should serve as an instrument for motivation; therefore, they should not be too difficult or easy to achieve. They should be fair to all parties concerned.

Performance objectives should be consistent with the available and anticipated resources of the school.

Objectives which require large expenditures of funds may be a waste of effort. Administrators have frequently maintained that if the funds were available, they could produce the desired results. However, in many cases, this has not occurred. Although administrators and teachers should be encouraged to develop creative objectives, they should be cautioned to be realistic about the acquisition of the necessary funds.

Performance objectives should avoid and/or minimize joint accountability.

The effectiveness of performance objectives is greatly reduced when accountability is shared by two parties. If the objectives cannot be subdivided and individual accountability designated, then all persons involved in the achievement of the objectives should be held accountable. Without individual accountability there is a tendency to duplicate effort.

CHARACTERISTICS OF WELL-DEFINED PERFORMANCE OBJECTIVES

When clearly defined goals are lacking, it is virtually impossible to evaluate a task or program efficiently and there is no sound basis for selecting alternatives, strategies, methods, techniques to achieve objectives. A meaningful performance objective should include the following three components: [1]

Statement of the Condition

The first component of a performance objective consists of a task statement of the conditions which identify the environment, resources, restraints, or limitations under which the person may perform the given act, such as the following: [2]

---

[1] James Lewis, Jr., *A Systems Approach to Developing Behavioral Objectives*, Northeast Association for the Individualization of Instruction, Wyandanch, N. Y., 1970.

[2] Long range goals do not usually include statement of the condition. This is amplified further in this chapter.

> With the assistance of the principals and curriculum associates . . .

Statement of the Act

The second component of a performance objective delineates in observable terms the specific act a person is required to perform in order to obtain a desired goal, i.e.:

> I will activate and chair a district-wide curriculum committee. . . .

Statement of Minimal Standards

The third component of a performance objective sets standards of acceptable performance or success criteria:

> This committee will meet a minimum of twice a month and have the responsibility for assessing the curriculum needs of the district and drawing up a detailed curriculum K-12, relevant to the educational needs of the Wyandanch children. By May 1, 1972, said curriculum is to be formalized.

Now that the three basic components of performance objectives have been identified and explained, the reader should try to recognize which one of the following two statements is expressed in terms of "observable action":

> I [*principal*] will have a better understanding of how to implement the nongraded concept in my building.
>
> I [*principal*] will write a procedural guideline for the implementation of the nongraded concept in my building.

The second statement states in observable terms what the principal will do. He will *write* a procedural guideline . . .

The first statement denotes that the principal will have a better understanding of how to implement the nongraded concept in the building. This statement is not clear. The reader is unable to state what the principal will do as a result of his understanding.

Which one of the following two statements of performance is stated in terms of observable action?

> I [*teacher*] will learn more about [*child's name*] through observation in free activity, busy activities, individual work periods and structural group activities.
>
> I [*teacher*] will have a better understanding of [*child's name*] through observing him in free activity, busy individual work periods and structural group activity.

Neither statement is stated correctly. The first statement that the teacher will learn about the student is rather vague and does not say what the teacher will be able to do as a result of the additional knowledge. The second statement also is vague and does not specify what will result after the teacher has acquired a better understanding of the child.

However, both of these vague statements can be salvaged by specifying in observable terms what the teacher will be able to do as a result of the additional knowledge and better understanding of the child.

The completed statement may look like the following:

> I [*teacher*] will learn more about [child's name] through observation in free activity, busy individual work periods and structural group activities so that I am able to:
>
> 1. *Identify* his interests and needs.
> 2. *Determine* what peers he gets along with best.
> 3. *Recognize* his idiosyncrasies.
> 4. *Identify* his particular problem areas.

The second statement can also be modified to be an acceptable objective statement by including everything after the words . . . so that . . .

It was mentioned previously that a well-defined performance objective should not only state the specific act to be performed but also the conditions. Following is one of the earliest statements concerning the nongraded concept:

> I [*principal*] will write a procedural guideline for the implementation of the nongraded concept.

It was also indicated previously that this statement *does* express the act to be performed in observable terms. Does this statement also specify the conditions under which the performance is to take place?

No it does not. İt cannot be determined from the statement whether the principal is going to visit nongraded schools across the country or attend a workshop on nongraded education. Each condition may be substantially different from the rest and may make certain unique demands upon the principal in order to achieve the objectives. By adding on a condition . . .

> After attending a three-week institute on nongraded education, I [*principal*] will be able to write a procedural guideline for the implementation of the nongraded concept in my building.

This objective now meets two of the three basic components of performance objectives.

To include a statement of condition in the second objective the following is added:

> During the next two weeks of school I [*teacher*] will learn more about [*child's name*] through observation.

It was mentioned previously that the third essential component of performance objectives is the setting of standards of acceptable performance or the success criteria.

Examine the following statement to determine if a statement describing minimal acceptable standards is delineated:

> I [*curriculum instruction intern*] will enroll in and successfully complete further courses in curriculum administration at Queens College, Flushing, New York, in the 1971 Fall semester. I shall take Ed. 776.1, Problems and Practices in Curriculum Development; Ed. 777.1, Guided Field Experience in Curriculum Development, for a total of four (4) credits. In the Spring semester, 1972, I shall take Ed. 776.2 and Ed. 777, Part II, for a total of four (4) additional credits. A minimum acceptable grade is B or better.

Does this statement establish a minimum standard of achievement? Yes, it does . . . "A minimum acceptable grade is B or better." Review the first objective in its revised form:

> After attending a three-week institute on the nongraded concept, I [*principal*] will write a procedural guideline for the implementation of the nongraded concept in my building.

Does this statement describe a minimal level of acceptable standards? No, it does not. However, by adding the following statement the objective will contain the three basic components:

> . . . which will be accepted by the teachers of my building and the administrative staff.

Examine the second statement in its revised form:

> During the next two weeks of school I [*teacher*] will learn more about [*child's name*] through observation in free activity, busy individual work periods and structured group activities so that I am able to:
>
> 1. *Identify* his interests and needs.
> 2. *Determine* what peers he gets along with.
> 3. *Recognize* his idiosyncrasies.
> 4. *Identify* his particular problem areas.

Does this statement establish a minimal standard of performance? Yes, it does. The statement describing the condition also describes the minimal level of performance in terms of a time limitation which in this case is . . . during the next two weeks of school.

WRITING MINIMAL STANDARDS TO MEASURE THE UNMEASURABLE

At times the reader will experience some degree of difficulty in writing minimal standards for certain statements which are stated in non-observable or unmeasurable terms. Some of the terms are denoted under "nonaction words" on page 80. For example, let us examine the phrase "to understand". If this phrase was used to develop a statement of the act of an objective, it would be difficult to state a standard for measuring results. That is, unless included in the statement, there is a description of what is meant by the term "to understand", so that the phrase will mean the same thing to every reader. It was Odiorne who stated, "If you can't *count* it, *measure* it, or *describe* it, you probably don't know what you want, and often can forget it as a goal."[3] The following is a guideline, developed by this author, which should prove valuable for writing minimal standards to measure the measurable.

1. It is often necessary to devise measurements of present levels in order to be able to estimate or calculate change from this level.
2. The most reliable measures are the real time or *hard* data in which the physical objects or tangible evidence comprise the measures to be used. (Academic achievement scores, days of attendance, etc.)
3. When *hard* data can't be used, an index or ratio is the next most accurate measure. This is an average, or per cent, a fraction or a ratio.
4. If neither of the above two can be used, a scale may be constructed. Such scales may be "rated from one to ten," a nominal rating against a check list of adjectives such as "excellent, fair, poor," or one which describes "better than" or "worse than" some arbitrary scale.
5. Verbal scales are the least precise, but can be extremely useful in identifying present levels and noting real change. Verbs such as "directs," "checks," and "reports" are indicative of action to be taken.
6. General descriptions are the least useful, but still have value in establishing benchmarks for change. "A clear, cloudless, fall day" is obviously not the same as a "cloudy, foggy, misty day" and the two descriptions could be used to state conditions as they exist and conditions as they should be.
7. The statements of measurements should be directed more toward output than toward activity. (Much activity may prove impossible to state in specific terms, whereas results of that activity can be so stated.)
8. In stating results sought or in defining present levels, effort should be made to find indicative, tangible levels and convert verbal or general descriptions into such tangible scales, ratios, or measures where possible.[4]

---

[3] George S. Odiorne, *Personnel Administration by Objectives*. Richard D. Irwin, Inc., Homewood, Ill., 1971, p. 119.

[4] *Ibid*. The author has substituted the word *hard* for *raw* in the original text of George S. Odiorne.

GUIDE TO DEVELOPING PERFORMANCE OBJECTIVES
IN OBSERVABLE TERMS

A meaningful stated performance objective is one that succeeds in communicating a performance intent. It is meaningful to the extent it conveys to the administrator a picture (of what a successful performance experience will be like) identical to the picture the teacher has in mind. Since a Statement of a Performance Objectives is a collection of words and symbols to express some action, it should be apparent that various combinations may be used to express a performance intent. The problem then emerges, how does one arrange words and symbols so that they will communicate a performance intent (objective) *exactly* like what the teacher (writer) has in mind? Although this problem is relatively simple, the best statement of performance objective is the one that delimits the greatest number of misinterpretations. However, experience has shown that initially most educators have had difficulties writing performance objectives in observable terms.

Earlier it was stated that objectives are written to express an action. The key word is action. All performance objectives should be written to include action verbs which can be evaluated in observable terms. Action words are open to fewer interpretations than non-action words. The following list contains a ready sampling of both:

Words Open to Many Interpretations (Non-action Words)	Words Open to Fewer Interpretations (Action Words)
to know	to list
to appreciate	to write
to understand	to compare
to comprehend	to select
to learn	to identify
to like	to compose
to value	to contrast
to believe	to solve
to enjoy	to differentiate

Important Consideration

The mere fact that a performance objective may be stated within a non-observable action term does not mean that the objective is poorly written. By qualifying the non-observable statement with observable statements, we transform a poorly designed statement of performance into an acceptable statement.

> I will encourage the building principals to strengthen the Parent-Teacher Association of their schools by:
>
> 1. Providing them with at least three techniques for increasing the attendance at PTA meetings;
> 2. Providing them with at least two methods of maintaining parental interest in the PTA meetings;
> 3. Providing them with five ways for securing funds for replenishing the PTA treasury;
> 4. Giving them three examples of possible projects which the PTA may wish to conduct during the school year;
> 5. Assisting them in arriving at an agenda for their next meeting.

Obviously by amending a poorly written statement of an objective with observable terms, the objective becomes measurable.

WRITING ACTION PLANS FOR PERFORMANCE OBJECTIVES

It was stated previously that a well-defined performance objective must contain the condition, an act, and a statement indicating minimal standards. This information is used as a base to guide the educator in the achievement of the performance objective. Although objectives delineate "specifics," a wide latitude of action for the educator still exists within the "specifics;" this will make it difficult for anyone to determine if the action will necessarily lead to the accomplishment of the objective. In order to alleviate this problem it is recommended that the educator write action plans for reaching the performance objective.

FACTORS TO CONSIDER WHEN DEVELOPING ACTION PLANS

Action plans are said to have been developed successfully when the performance objective has been achieved. In order to enhance the probability for achieving an objective, there are some essential factors, such as the following, which should be considered when writing action plans:

1. They should be realistic and attainable.
2. They should be specific as to exactly what is to be accomplished.

3 . They should describe activities leading to achievement of objectives.
4 . They should contain specific target dates.
5 . They should be listed in sequential order leading to the achievement of the objectives.

The following is a sample of a performance objective and an action plan:

Short-Range Objective:

Assisted by a representative from each building, I will publish, for in-district use, a complete inventory of textbook holdings, by title, by location, annotation to include publisher, date and series. Distribution is to be ready by January 1, 1972.

Action Plan:

1 . Conduct a meeting with all building representatives and brief them on their task assignment, identify their individual responsibility to this assignment, and explain the format for compiling the inventory.
   Target date: September 15, 1971.
2 . Secure up-to-date inventories from each building representative.
   Target date: October 15, 1971.
3 . Complete and integrate the lists.
   Target date: October 30, 1971.
4 . Ascertain from the district coordinator a preferred form for final typing.
   Target date: November 20, 1971.
5 . Arrange for typing and reproduction.
   Target date: December 1, 1971.
6 . Deliver to curriculum coordinator for distribution.
   Target date: December 21, 1971.

VALUE OF CITING ACTION PLANS

When the process of school management by objectives is implemented, control in the operation of the school is maintained by measuring performance. Performance is measured by evaluating the sub-series of steps which lead to the resultant action. By reviewing this sub-series of steps, the following additional advantages are accrued:

Action plans are means for—

1. determining whether or not an objective will be achieved.
2. determining the relative values of the work performed in order to reach an objective.
3. measuring individual performances.
4. self-evaluating and correcting performance.
5. making future predictions.
6. making contributions and consistent re-evaluation of methods, techniques and results.
7. comparing the performance of the educators, teams, departments and schools.
8. focusing on all aspects of the job.
9. improving basic attitudes of educators in the pursuit of an objective.

CONSTRAINTS ON ACTION PLANS

Before any action plans are constructed, the educator should consider the possible constraints which may have an effect on the achievement of the objective. Once this determination is made, the teacher or administrator can then proceed to develop realistic and meaningful action plans for achieving performance objectives.

The following is a list of constraints which must be considered when establishing action plans:

1. Availability of Funds

Under this constraint, it willl be necessary to determine whether funds are available to achieve the objective. Questions which should be given some considerations are: Are funds needed in order to achieve this performance objective? If so, will the funds come from the general budget, federal funds or local sources? What must be accomplished in order to acquire these funds?

2. Time Element

The time element is an important factor to the achievement of any objective. Questions which should be considered are: Is time an essential factor for achieving these objectives? If so, how much time is needed in order to advance toward achieving the objectives?

3. Availability of Curriculum Materials and Supplies

Availability of materials and supplies may affect achievement of objectives. Thought should be given to: Are curriculum materials and supplies needed in order to accomplish the objective? If so, what materials and supplies are needed? Will the materials and supplies presently available in this school suffice? Must they be supplemented?

4. Personnel Training

The teacher or administrator who is developing the action plan must consider questions pertaining to special training if necessary, to achievement: Is the present staff adequately trained to perform this objective? If not, what kind of training program must be established to get that staff trained? How will we be able to get staff and operation in the training exercise? How much time will be needed for training the staff?

5. Student Participation

The need for involving students is particularly great in the secondary school. Throughout the country, secondary students are demanding a greater voice in the affairs of the schools. Teachers set objectives to improve student performance. It is only natural that students have something to say about the objectives teachers set for them. Questions which should be considered are: How do we get maximum participation from the students? In what way should students be involved?

6. Community Participation

Parents, who make up a large portion of the community, have the same goals for their youngsters as the public schools. Often, however, parents and other members of the community don't know how to reach these goals. Public schools have not been as responsive to community participation as they should be because they often fail or neglect to involve them in the affairs of the school district. For this reason, certain programs and changes have met with resistance and in some cases outright rejection. The following questions should be considered in order to judge the need for community participation:

Will the achievement of the objectives call for major changes? Is community participation required by board policy or federal regulations? Will the success of the objectives hinge on community participation? Has a local Parent Advisory Council been established to ensure community participation?

7. Attitude of Staff

The attitude of the staff may be a factor to be reckoned with in order to achieve the objective. Questions which should be considered are: Will the staff be receptive to the objective? If not, what would be the most effective way to get staff acceptance?

8. Staff Involvement and Participation

If the attitude of the staff is going to be a serious factor in the successful achievement of the objective, it may be necessary or even mandatory to get staff participation in the achievement of the objectives. Questions which should be given some consideration are: How should the staff be involved? To what extent should the staff participate? Are incentives necessary to encourage participation?

9. Policy, Procedure Constraints or Contractual Agreement

There may be certain policy, procedure or contractual agreement constraints which may be opposed to the objectives and constitute an obstacle to its achievement. If this is the case, the objective and/or action plans must either be revised or special permission must be granted to circumvent those obstacles which may prevent the achievement of the objective.

10. Availability of Resources

The availability of resources such as personnel, equipment, supplies, materials and fixtures usually affects the accomplishment of most objectives. Therefore the educator must know what resources are available and proceed to achieve the objectives within the limitation of constraints imposed by these items.

11. Methods and Techniques

The question of whether new methods and techniques are needed to advance toward the achievement of the objective must be considered. There may be special methods and techniques to be learned. If this is the case, the acquisition of this method or technique becomes a constraint which must be satisfied in order to achieve the objective.

12. Environmental Constraints

Environmental constraints refer to the available facilities which may be necessary for advancement toward the achievement of the objective. Facilities include those items by and within which the educator will perform in an attempt to meet the objective.

By determining which of the constraints and limitations will offset the fulfillment of our objectives, we will establish our standards for the objectives. By working within the frame of our constraints and limitations, we directly affect "what" we are going to do and "how" we are going to do it.

The prime purpose of action plans is to serve as an indicator of successful performance. Failure to meet a particular action plan is a red light that says that the teacher or administrator is off track and unless the educator gets "on track" by meeting certain predetermined plans, the objectives will not be met. Action plans demand a great deal of thinking through before they are developed. Many plans can be established for a single performance objective. The individual educator must apply his own knowledge and judgment together with that of other educators to develop a realistic and attainable action plan in the pursuit of an objective.

WRITING LONG RANGE GOALS AND SHORT RANGE OBJECTIVES

Long Range Goals

Long range goals are broad task assignments to be achieved over a period of three years or more. They should be specific and measurable. There are also long range plans destined to achieve school district's organizational objectives. The condition under which the goal will be achieved is usually omitted from long range goals. Each long range goal should begin with "to increase, to decrease, to provide, etc.". Also, each long range goal should state the "from _____ and to _____ and over ___(period)___." Two examples of long range goals are as follows:

> To reduce the absentee rate of teachers from 1700 days per year to 850 days per year (50%) over a three-year period (1971-74).
>
> To increase the rate of high school seniors enrolling in college from 50% to 90% over a four-year period (1971-75).

Sometimes long range goals are stated with constraints, such as the following:

Long Range Goal:

> To increase the number of primary students in the Martin Luther King Elementary School who are on grade level in reading from 23% to 80% or more over a three-year period (1970-73).

Standard: (Constraint)

> As identified by any series of the Metropolitan Achievement Test.

Short Range Objectives

Short range objectives are specific performance objectives, usually achieved over a period of one year for the purpose of progressing toward the long range goal, such as the following:

Short Range Objective:

> Utilizing the service of Mr. George Cureton, Reading Consultant for the School District, I (principal) will implement the Cureton Reading Program in my building during the school year 1971-72 and increase the percentage of students on grade level in reading from 23% to 50%, as measured by the Metropolitan Achievement Test.

Action Plans:

1. Complete the training of all teachers in the Cureton Reading Program by August 30, 1971.
2. Assist teachers in the development and completion of all materials and institutional tools for use in the Cureton Reading Program by August 30, 1971.

3. Assist teachers in administrating and scoring pre-test MAT—Series A on September 20, 1971.
4. Conduct daily tour of classes to assist individual teachers with the Cureton Reading Program.
5. Assisted by Mr. Cureton, conduct problem-solving conference on Cureton Reading Program every other Monday at 2:45 p.m.
6. Assisted by the director of curriculum and instruction, check each class profile sheet by the last school day of each month.
7. Assisted by the teacher, administer and score the Standard Achievement Test in Reading to all students by January 15, 1972.
8. Utilizing the results from the Standard Achievement Test, teacher will diagnose and prescribe additional work for students not on grade level.
9. Assist teachers in administering and scoring the Metropolitan Achievement Test—Series B by April 30, 1972.
10. Report the results of the pre- and post-tests to the chief school officer by May 1, 1972.

SUMMARY

The writing of objectives is perhaps the most critical activity to be achieved in the performance appraisal program. The values of writing performance objectives are: (1) provide a clear focus for performance activity; (2) provide a means by which the educational leader and the educator enter into a contract for performance; (3) induce decision making; (4) provide a more efficient and effective utilization of time and effort; (5) assess performance periodically; (6) help to fix in the minds of school personnel their individual objectives; (7) help to judge the school's effectiveness; (8) play an important part in training and development; (9) use as a basis for motivation; (10) use to improve educational leader-educator relationships. The four basic components of objectives are: (1) the condition which specifies people, environment, restraints, resources or limitations affecting the objectives to be performed; (2) the act which states in observable terms restraints, resources or limitations affecting the objectives to be performed; (3) the act which states in observable terms what is to be performed and when; (4) the success criteria which specify minimal levels of performance. Performance objectives must be written so that the act specifies in observable terms the exact task a person is required to perform in order to obtain a desired goal.

Action plans are individual statements of personal commitment to take steps specifically designed to accomplish a performance objective. There are five factors to consider when developing action plans. They should be: (1) realistic and obtainable; (2) specific; (3) activity-oriented to achieve the objective; (4) specific in stating target dates; (5) listed in sequential order. There are several constraints which should be taken into consideration when developing action plans. These are: (1) availability of funds; (2) time element; (3) availability of curriculum materials and supplies; (4) personnel training; (5) community participation; (6) attitude of staff; (7) staff involvement and participation; (8) policies, procedures and contractual agreements; (9) availability of resources; (10) methods and techniques; and (11) environmental constraints. Long range goals are broad objectives to be achieved over three years or more. Short range objectives are designed to progress toward the achievement of long range goals in one year or less.

FIVE

Developing Professional Skill Objectives

Numerous attempts have been made to predict teacher effectiveness (Anderson and Hunka, 1963; Biddle, 1964; Turner and Faitu, 1960). However, very little progress has been made in this area, perhaps due to the method by which the problem has been conceptualized. Most researchers have either explicitly or implicitly assumed the existence of a single set of criteria as to what constitutes the effective teacher. To add injury to an open wound, the teacher is then subjectively evaluated by the principal, using the set of criteria as a guide. Many administrators have assumed that these criteria are absolute and that they can be used effectively by any administrator in any school and under any conditions. The author has attempted in this chapter to illustrate how a set of criteria can be used not to evaluate teachers' effectiveness, but to *assess* their performance in order to pinpoint areas needing improvement. Armed with this information, the teacher can then set professional skill objectives to improve his performance. The rationale for the chapter is to define professional skill objectives, to state the importance of professional skill objectives, to identify attributes of professional skill objectives, to define the professional skill check list, to describe the mechanics of the evaluation procedures for teachers and administrators, to explain the reverberational effects of unachieved professional skill objectives and to delineate the construction of problem-solving objectives.

DEFINING PROFESSIONAL SKILL OBJECTIVES

Professional skill objectives are clearly defined statements describing critical aspects of typical administrative or teaching performance. They may be referred to as the "basic requirements" for effective administration or teaching. Thus, the main function of professional skill objectives is to project a plan for an educator to perform adequately on the job in order to maintain the status quo. If these required objectives are not satisfactorily achieved and maintained according to a mutually agreed upon time and extent, the educational program suffers and the school district begins to decline in efficiency of operations. All other objectives are subordinate to professional skill objectives. This point is vividly demonstrated in Figure 5-1, the Priorities of Objectives.

THE IMPORTANCE OF STATING PROFESSIONAL SKILL OBJECTIVES

It has been stated earlier by the author that the present attempts to formally evaluate teachers have been instrumental in perpetuating the mistrust that has developed over a period of years between administrators and teachers. The problem then is that neither teachers, supervisors nor administrators are provided with clearly defined directions in terms of professional skills and thus are not cognizant of the various tasks expected of them. Likewise, other school personnel such as teacher aides, superintendent of grounds, transportation supervisors, etc., are not provided with objective job statements spelling out in specific terms what is actually expected of them. It is obvious then that some new method of measuring and evaluating school personnel performance is necessary. Any new method must be adaptable to the roles and responsibilities of all school personnel, depending less upon methods and techniques used by school personnel and depending more on the evaluation of the results achieved in relation to the task performed. The author does not mean to imply that methods and techniques are unimportant, but merely to emphasize that the methods or techniques used may or may not get the desired results. At the same time, educators cannot continue to evaluate performance based on "inaction" methods and techniques.

To ensure educational accountability, task performance must be assessed and then evaluated against some sort of predescribed "success criteria" for which any number of school personnel can share a common responsibility. Where there are objectives, the success criteria should be developed and individual responsibility should be identified and explained. The individual should be charged only with that prorata share of the common objectives which pertains to his individual assignment.

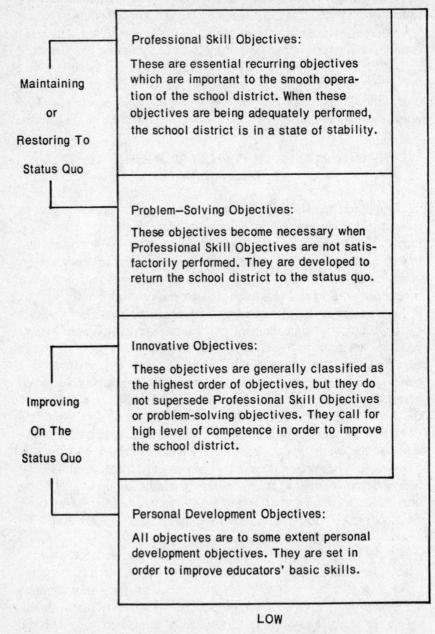

HIGH

Professional Skill Objectives:

These are essential recurring objectives which are important to the smooth operation of the school district. When these objectives are being adequately performed, the school district is in a state of stability.

Problem—Solving Objectives:

These objectives become necessary when Professional Skill Objectives are not satisfactorily performed. They are developed to return the school district to the status quo.

Innovative Objectives:

These objectives are generally classified as the highest order of objectives, but they do not supersede Professional Skill Objectives or problem-solving objectives. They call for high level of competence in order to improve the school district.

Personal Development Objectives:

All objectives are to some extent personal development objectives. They are set in order to improve educators' basic skills.

Maintaining

or

Restoring To

Status Quo

Improving

On The

Status Quo

LOW

Figure 5-1 THE PRIORITIES OF OBJECTIVES

All school personnel should include professional skill objectives in their statements of performance objectives which must be specifically delineated for the following reasons as explained by Odiorne.

> The *administrator* should be cognizant of the small things that preoccupy the teachers. Though the *administrator* often isn't even aware of these routine operations, they may be important in that failure to do them well could have serious consequences, whereas, when they are well done their effect is apparently invisible.
>
> Routine matters are often loss-prevention actions that avert the larger attention that will be needed later if they are poorly executed.
>
> In estimating the distribution of duties among his various staff members, the *administrator* needs to be cognizant of this routine work in order to estimate the coverage of all of the facets of the operation, and the management of the time of his *teachers*.
>
> In deciding on the distribution of the work these routine duties must first be spelled out. Such statements then form the basis for a more orderly clustering of duties to allow for their most effective performance.[1]

Although some schools have made it a practice not to list professional skill objectives, this author disapproves of this practice and maintains that these objectives which are vital to the stability of a school district cannot be taken for granted and must be indicated in writing.

George L. Morrisey confirms the importance of listing professional skill objectives by stating:

> There is a tendency in much of the emphasis on objectives to concentrate primarily on new or innovative activities. But to be meaningful, objectives must include the normal work output of the unit as well. Far too many "objectives" that are written today take on the aspect of special projects which have a tendency to fall by the wayside when the going gets rough.[2]

An educator's job description may contain hundreds of performance tasks, each to be developed into a professional skill objective. It is highly recommended that the instrument for assessing professional

---

[1] George S. Odiorne, *Management by Objectives*. Pitman Publishing Corp., New York, N.Y., 1965, p. 103. The author has substituted the word *administrator* for *boss* and *superior* and *teaches* for *subordinates* in the original text of George S. Odiorne.

[2] George L. Morrisey, *Management by Objectives and Results*. Addison Wesley, Reading, Mass., 1970, p. 40.

skills be listed according to priority sequence, in a terse manner, and in a check list form. Constructing professional skills in check list form will serve as an invaluable aid to new teachers and teachers who are performing below par and will provide a basis for developing performance objectives for improving those items designated as needing improvement.

IDENTIFYING ATTRIBUTES OF PROFESSIONAL SKILL OBJECTIVES

There are some attributes of professional skill objectives which are called to the attention of the reader.

1. Professional skill objectives are regular duties and may not entail creativity or innovation on the job.

2. Salary for any school position is based upon the achievement of professional skill objectives and should never be considered for extra pay such as bonus, merit and incentive. Any additional compensation beyone the regular salary should be for performing beyond these objectives.

3. Dismissal or relocation is likely to occur if professional skill objectives are not performed according to accepted levels of performance. A person who repeatedly fails to discharge his professional skill objectives as agreed is incompetent and his use to the school district should be seriously questioned.

DEFINING THE PROFESSIONAL SKILL CHECK LIST

The Professional Skill Check List is a basic criteria guide which describes general assumptions about the main areas of concern regarding effective teaching, supervision and administration. It is used as an assessment guide to common understanding between an educator and his immediate supervisor. Although this evaluation guide is to some extent subjective, its function is to focus intelligent, informed and experienced judgment of an educator's performance in critical areas. When followed by explicit and objective goal setting that reinforces strengths and improves the weakness, improved performance is a natural result.

On the following pages is an example of a Professional Skill Check List for assessing teacher performance. It is used by the Westport Public Schools, Westport, Conn., and has been modified by the author.

PROFESSIONAL SKILL CHECK LIST FOR ASSESSING
TEACHER'S EFFECTIVENESS

TEACHER Mrs. Mary Wilkerson *	DATE: September 15, 1972
SCHOOL: Milton Olive Elem. School	PRINCIPAL: Mr. James Butler

The following check list is to be used as a guideline for assessing the effectiveness of teachers. Only those items receiving "needs improvement" and which have been mutually agreed to are to be developed and used as a basis for setting professional skill objectives and evaluating performance.

Professional Skills	Appropriate	Needs Improvement
1. Presents subject matter in a logical form, stressing the higher thought processes.	X	
2. Demonstrates mastery of subject matter for grade or subject.	X	
3. Demonstrates effective long-range course planning.	X	
4. Demonstrates effective daily or short-term planning.	X	
5. Coordinates planning and preparation of classroom and materials.	X	
6. Maintains a favorable classroom environment (psychological) for learning.		X

* Those items designated "needs improvement" are used as the basis for developing the professional skills objectives of the Statement of Performance Objectives illustrated in Chapter Eight.

Professional Skills	Appropriate	Needs Improvement
7. Maintains a classroom environment (physical) conducive to learning.		X
8. Demonstrates fairness and kindness in dealing with students.		X
9. Varies methods to suit topic or pupil.	X	
10. Varies instructional materials to suit topic or pupil.		X
11. Makes effective and differentiated assignments.	X	
12. Plans for and meets the needs of individual students.	X	
13. Uses suitable pupil evaluation procedures.	X	
14. Demonstrates a respect for the integrity of the individual pupil personality.	X	
15. Demonstrates intelligent economy in the use of materials and equipment.	X	
16. Seeks to instill moral and ethical values.	X	
17. Is receptive to intelligent educational experimentation.	X	
18. Displays a contagious enthusiasm for knowledge.	X	
19. Assigns homework with respect of the stu-		

	Appropriate	Needs Improvement
dents out of school time.	X	
20. Initiates problem-solving conference to solve student or class problems.		X
21. Provides structure within a "free" environment for learning.	X	
22. Provides a variety of learning materials and equipment to encourage self-directed learning.	X	
23. Communicates effectively with students.		X

Staff Relationship	Appropriate	Needs Improvement
24. Works cooperatively with staff members toward attaining the goals accepted for the schools and department.	X	
25. Participates willingly in grade conferences, committee work and team or department meetings.	X	
26. Works willingly with study groups and curriculum committee.	X	
27. Displays loyalty to the school and community.	X	
28. Complies with school regulations regarding absenteeism, tardiness, meetings, committees,		

Staff Relationship	Appropriate	Needs Improvement
reports and assign-ments.	X	
29. Works cooperatively with teachers and ad-ministratively toward attaining objectives of the school district, school building, team or department.	X	

Professional Development	Appropriate	Needs Improvement
30. Takes personal respon-sibility for individual professional growth.	X	
31. Participates in profes-sional organizations.	X	
32. Initiates a variety of personal development activities.	X	

Parents and Community Relations	Appropriate	Needs Improvement
33. Takes appropriate ac-tion in regard to par-ents' requests, com-plaints and concerns.	X	
34. Displays a willingness to explain classroom procedures and educa-tional programs.		X
35. Displays effectiveness in parent-teacher con-ferences.	X	
36. Attends parent-teacher association meetings.	X	

37. Avoids argumentation or defensive attitude with parents.	X	
38. Cooperates effectively with parents on conference follow-up.	X	
39. Participates effectively in a number of community affairs or projets.	X	

MECHANICS OF THE EVALUATION PROCEDURES FOR TEACHERS AND ADMINISTRATORS

The mechanics of the evaluation procedure for teachers illustrated in Figure 5-2 are explained as follows:

1. A committee of teachers establishes a list of basic criteria for assessing professional skills of teachers. Each item is to be assessed for "appropriate" and "needs improvement."
2. The list of basic criteria for assessing professional skills of teachers is reviewed by the principal. Adjustments are made as warranted. The final list is mutually agreed to by the principal and teachers' committee. The list of basic criteria then becomes a "contract" between the principal and each teacher. The list is *not* to be used as an evaluative instrument.
3. Using the list of basic criteria, the teacher initiates self assessment. The principal initiates his own assessment of the teacher's performance using the list of basic criteria as his guide.
4. Principal and teacher confer to mutually agree to the items or areas needing improvement. Both parties reach an understanding about the objectives which are to be developed by the teacher.
5. Using the list of basic criteria as a guideline and the information mutually agreed to in the conference, the teacher develops objectives and action plans in the form of a Statement of Performance Objectives to improve performance in the areas needing improvement. Each item designated "needs improvement" is covered by an objective.
6. Principal reviews the teacher's proposed objectives. Objec-

tives may be modified, revised or deleted. New objectives
may be added. All objectives must be mutually agreed to
by both parties concerned.

7 . Teacher exerts efforts to achieve objectives in accordance
with mutually agreed upon plans.

8 . Teacher initiates self-evaluation by using his Statement of
Performance Objectives as a guide and records the outcome
of performance on a professional performance review form.
The principal initiates an evaluation of the teacher's performance. Principal and teacher reach an understanding and mutually agree to modify, revise, and/or delete objectives. New
objectives may be added. This particular step is initiated
from two to four times a year for each teacher.

The mechanics of the evaluation procedure for administrators is
almost identical to that of the teachers. The only difference is that
instead of a committee of administrators developing the professional
skill criteria for assessing administrators' performances, each administrator develops his own criteria, which is mutually agreed to by his
immediate supervisor.

THE REVERBERATIONAL EFFECTS OF UNACHIEVED
PROFESSIONAL SKILL OBJECTIVES

Whenever professional skill objectives of administrators are not
achieved, they inevitably create reverberations which may bring
on chain reactions which can have numerous grave consequences.

Each professional skill objective for a school system is similar
in structure and importance to each vertebra of the backbone of the
human body. If one vertebra is immobilized, the movement of the
human body may be seriously impaired, causing certain painful or par-
alytic conditions. If one or more professional skill objectives of
administrators are not achieved, the stability of the school district
may be impaired, creating such conditions as reprimands, loss of
funds, dismissals, etc. Take, for example, the true situation described
below:

A superintendent of a small suburban school in a poor black
community received a call from the ESEA Title I Office of the
State Education Department inquiring as to the disposition of

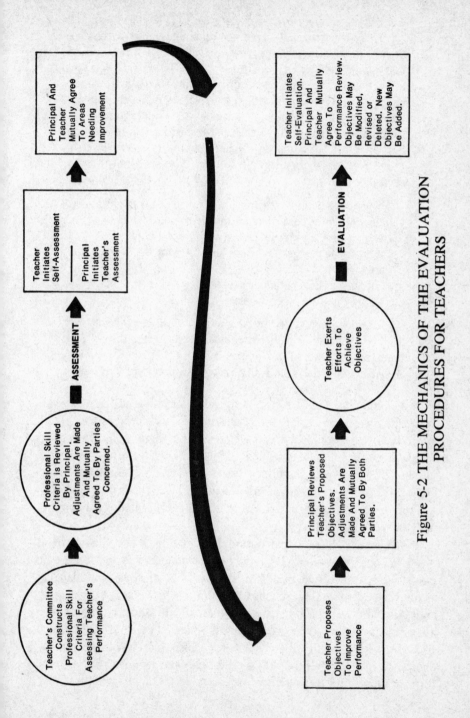

Figure 5-2 THE MECHANICS OF THE EVALUATION PROCEDURES FOR TEACHERS

the end-of-the-year report for last year's Title I Project. The superintendent said that he did not know that the report had not been submitted on time, and apologetically stated that he would look into the matter and report back to the Title I Office within a few hours. The chief school officer immediately called in the business manager and asked him to explain why the above mentioned form had not been submitted to the State Education Department on time. The business manager responded that he was too busy (performing a number of other tasks) to complete the end-of-the-year report for the Title I Office. The business manager cited the following:

- Negotiated with the teacher aides for the board of education.
- Attended three conferences related to business administration.
- Took a few days from accrued vacation time.
- Worked on budget of a new project with the high school principal.
- Interviewed several applicants.
- Various regular other duties.

An investigation revealed that due to the lack of compliance with the state regulations concerning federal funds, the district had to borrow $1,400,000.00 at the rate of 6¼% to meet salary demands under the Title I proposal over a period of two years.

An examination of this case is revealing. First of all, the business manager was negligent in performing his professional skill objectives. Complying with state and federal regulations concerning funds is an ordinary duty which should take top priority. Secondly, the business manager performed certain personal development objectives at the expense of professional skill objectives. The effect of this unachieved professional skill objective had far-reaching, deleterious consequences.

If the superintendent had periodically reviewed the Statement of Performance Objectives with his business manager, this problem would probably not have occurred. Needless to say, the business manager should have fulfilled his regular duties in the first place.

If this information had reached the board of education, an explanation from the superintendent would be in order. The nonfulfillment of this professional skill objective is just cause for the business manager's dismissal, that is, he should lose the opportunity to perform in the school district.

PROBLEM-SOLVING OBJECTIVES

Problem-solving objectives or emergency objectives usually evolve when professional skill objectives of administrators are not being met. The goal of problem-solving objectives then is to solve the problem in order to bring the school district back to its regular maintenance level, thereby re-establishing the status quo of the school district. When the problem-solving objective has been achieved, it is customary to include it into the professional skill objectives so that it becomes an ongoing part of the educator's ordinary and regular duties.

CONSTRUCTING PROBLEM-SOLVING OBJECTIVES

There are essentially three component parts to developing a statement of a problem-solving objective:

1. Identification of the Problem

The problem should be stated tersely and in precise terms. Because problem-solving objectives are developed to restore the school district back to the status quo, the statement of the problem should delineate a comparison between what is desired (status quo) and what is presently occurring to indicate the problem.

2. Statement of the Objective

After all of the possible alternative approaches to the solution of the problem have been considered, the best or most appropriate alternative should be used as the basis for developing an objective for solving the problem. There should also be included a statement indicating when the objective is a realistic goal, an optimistic goal, and a pessimistic goal.

3. Description of a Plan of Action

Once the objective has been developed, a plan of action must be constructed for the purpose of delineating procedural steps for achieving the objective and solving the problem. Each step in the plan of action should also contain an estimated time of completion.

The following is an example of a problem-solving objective:

Problem:

The school district has a budget deficit of $468,047.00 which must be reduced to zero by June 30, 1975 (4 years).

Objective:

To prepare and supervise a budget reduction program to reduce this amount from $468,047.00 to $318,047.00.

1. *Realistic Goal*:

   $150,000.00 was saved in 1970-71 and should be attainable this year.

2. *Optimistic Goal*:

   Increased availability of federal aid funds could provide an increase in savings as high as $200,000.00.

3. *Pessimistic Goal*:

   Anything lower than a $100,000.00 saving should be considered a failure for this objective.

Action Plan:

1. Review budget to identify areas of variable cost which can be altered. (9/1/71)
2. Estimate amounts by budget codes where proposed expenditures can be curtailed. (9/10/71)
3. Submit plan to the chief school officer for review and approval. (9/15/71)
4. Meet individually with building principals and supervisors to review plan. (9/15/71-9/30/71)
5. Adopt plan and put budgetary controls into effect. (10/1/71)
6. Report monthly progress to the chief school officer. (15th day of the following month.)
7. Meet with building principals and supervisors to discuss status of plan and remedies for special needs which may arise as a result of adoption of the plan. (As required.)
8. Report results of plan to staff. (7/31/72)

SUMMARY

Professional Skill Objectives are clearly defined statements describing critical aspects of typical administrative or teaching performance. The importance of stating professional skill objectives rests with the fact that to ensure educational accountability, task performance must be assessed and then evaluated against some sort of predescribed "success criteria" for which any number of school personnel can share a common responsibility. The attributes of stating professional skill objectives are:

1. They are regular duties and may not entail innovation on the job.
2. Salary for any position is based upon professional skill objectives.
3. Dismissal or relocation is likely to occur if professional skill objectives are not achieved.

The Professional Skill Check List is an assessment criteria guide which describes general assumption of main areas of concern regarding effective teaching, supervision and administration. Major categories in the professional skill check list are: (1) professional skills; (2) staff relationship; (3) professional development; (4) parent and community relations.

The mechanics of the evaluation procedures for teachers and administrators are:

1. Committee of teachers construct basic criteria for assessing professional skills.
2. The skill check list is mutually agreed to by the principal and teacher.
3. Using the skill check list the teacher initiates self-assessment. The principal initiates his own assessment of the teacher's performance.
4. The two parties mutually agree to the areas needing improvement.
5. Teacher develops objectives to improve performance in the areas needing improvement.
6. Objectives are reviewed by the principal. Adjustments are made and mutually agreed to by both parties.
7. Teacher exerts efforts to achieve objectives.
8. Teacher initiates self-evaluation. Teacher and principal mutually agree to teacher's performance outcome. Objectives may be modified, revised, deleted or added.

The mechanics of the evaluation procedures for administrators are identical to those of the teacher's except that the administrator develops his own basic criteria of professional skills instead of a committee. When professional skill objectives are not achieved, they create reverberations which may have grave consequences. When professional skill objectives are not achieved, they create the need for problem-solving objectives. There are three components to problem-solving objectives: (1) identification of the problem; (2) statement of the objective; (3) description of the action plan.

SIX

Setting Innovative Objectives

As long as children enter the portals of our schools, educators cannot afford to be satisfied with the status quo. Neither can they be satisfied with how the schools were operating in yesteryears. Changing times bring on changing conditions. Changing conditions mean that capable educators must constantly be on the alert seeking new ideas, new methods and new techniques to meet changing conditions. Administrators and supervisors who are reluctant to rock the boat and to effect constructive changes for improved education must give way to administrators and supervisors who are willing to assume risk in the interests of children. Teachers who have remained unmoved by innovations must understand the importance of implementing creative activities for improving the performance of youngsters. Administrators, supervisors and teachers must think and plan together and set objectives that will facilitate the learning process and lead to improving education for students. The purposes of this chapter are to define innovative objectives, to state the importance for delineating innovative objectives, to mention how to develop objectives for intrinsic innovation, to introduce extrinsic innovative activities, to enumerate the time interval for specifying objectives, to expound on some rules for introducing change in the school, to discuss some common errors in setting objectives, and to focus on the role of educational leaders in developing innovative objectives.

DEFINING INNOVATIVE OBJECTIVES

Innovative objectives are the highest order of objectives. These objectives are quantum breakthroughs in educational improvement rather than restorational oriented. They are quite different from professional skill objectives. The latter are designed to maintain the status quo, the former are designed to improve on the status quo. Innovative objectives are developed under the assumption that even if an educator achieves 100 per cent of his professional skill objectives, this is not enough. Innovative objectives further assume that professional skill, problem-solving objectives are merely necessary steps for maintaining the school district at a stable level.[1]

Innovative objectives are the most difficult to measure but they contribute to the improvement of the school through innovation and change. This means that educators may need to look within to effect creative ferment as well as introduce new ideas observed in other school districts. This means that educators must keep abreast of new developments. This means that educators must make feasibility studies to determine if selected innovations would work in their particular situation. This also means that educators must make intelligent, aggressive decisions, move for the implementation of new programs and make them work.

In essence, an innovative objective is a statement of an educational activity designed to improve present conditions and/or performance. The innovative objective could be one designed by a classroom teacher to establish a biology lab to improve students' achievement in biology or one designed by a principal to implement computer-assisted instruction in order to individualize instruction. Innovative objectives may be simple or complex in nature, may cover short or long durations, may be teaching or administrating-oriented, and may be designed for individual or group achievement.

THE IMPORTANCE OF STATING INNOVATIVE OBJECTIVES

No school person should be permitted to develop his own objectives on the basis that the status quo will suffice. The constant efforts to improve the status quo or to solve perennial problems is a professional responsibility and obligation which no dedicated and serious-minded educator can ignore. Innovative objectives for all professional employees of the school are important for the survival of the school and should be mandatory.

---

[1] George S. Ordione, *Management Decisions by Objectives*, Prentice-Hall, Inc., Englewood Cliffs, N.J., 1969, pp. 22-23.

The importance of expecting innovative objectives on the part of all school employees bears emphasis and repetition:

1. The school person who constantly fails to develop innovative objectives is merely maintaining the status quo of his position and therefore should not be considered for promotion, merit pay, bonuses, special considerations such as conference visitations (expenses paid by the district), sabbatical leave and salary increases other than the general salary increases.
2. The school person who fails to perform professional skill objectives adequately or to make an attempt to improve his job performance should be replaced or dismissed.
3. The school person who fails to perform his innovative objectives should not be penalized as severely as those school persons who fail to achieve professional skill objectives. The rate of failure for achieving innovative objectives is much higher than that of professional skill or personal development objectives and allowances should be made for this high attrition rate.
4. The school person who constantly takes advantage of circumstances and opportunities for improving his performance through innovative objectives should be supported and encouraged to continue.

MAJOR CATEGORIES OF OBJECTIVES

Innovation objectives fall into either of two major categories:[2]

1. Intrinsic. The discovery within the school of new ideas, activities, methods, techniques or systems for improving the performance of one or more tasks involving the school and the activities.

2. Extrinsic. A new idea or activity which is introduced from a source outside of the school in order to improve the performance of the school.

DEVELOPING OBJECTIVES FOR INTRINSIC INNOVATION

Although the introduction of innovation practices is important to improve performance, it has an interesting by-product. In order to

---

[2] George S. Ordione, *Management by Objectives, A System of Managerial Leadership*, Pitman Publishing Corp., New York, N.Y., 1965, p. 113.

effect changes, the innovator must discuss present conditions, and in doing so, he develops objectives in a systematic manner.

When the administrator and teacher confer to develop objectives, it is appropriate to critique past performance. However, if administrators commit one or more of the following errors during the negotiation session on objectives, the effectiveness of school management by objectives will be seriously hampered:

> The *administrator* decides to practice some amateur psychotherapy and alter the personality of the *teacher*.
>
> The *administrator* uses this occasion to apply pressure, basing his action on the presumption that "motivation" means stirring the *teacher* into faster action.
>
> The *administrator* confines the discussion to a mutual analysis of results, instead of leading the *teacher* into a more precise analysis of the situation, and the development of goals for better results in a systematic, insightful way.[3]

The negotiation session on objectives between the administrator and the teacher will pay off in the long run if both of these people think about the results obtained in the past for the purpose of improving on the present performance. The following series of stages for analyzing the situation is recommended.

1. Each participant (administrators, supervisors and teachers) should collect and research all the available data relating to the new idea activity. The collected data which each party may possess should be shared with all parties so that an intelligent decision can be made concerning the innovation and the formulation of the objectives. Both the teacher and administrator may have some information that the other does not have or which one might wish the other to know. This information could possibly include special problems in implementation cost, training of personnel, reluctance of the staff to accept the innovation, parental and student participation, board of education acceptance, etc.

2. After analyzing the situation, the problem should be analyzed to find out the reason for its existence and to speculate on the effects it will have if not solved.

---

[3] *Ibid.*, pp. 111-117. The author has substituted the word *administrator* for *superior* and the word *teacher* for *subordinate* in the original text of George S. Ordione.

3. The above data should then be analyzed. A decision is made for solving this particular type of problem which takes us to the next stage.

INTRODUCING EXTRINSIC ACTIVITIES

Most extrinsic innovative activities or ideas which have been implemented by forward-moving schools have been developed by persons, organizations or associations outside of the school. Some examples are: Individually Prescribed Instruction was developed by the University of Pittsburgh in conjunction with the Research for Better Schools; Westinghouse is credited with devising Project Plan; the nongraded concept was developed by Drs. John Goodlad and Robert Anderson; Program Planning and Budgeting Systems was adopted from business; British Infant School originated in England; differentiated staffing is credited to Dr. Dwight Allen of University of Massachusetts; and school management by objectives was adopted from business management techniques.

The school personnel elect to introduce new ideas into a school; they do not necessarily have to be the originators. In fact, most extrinsically-created ideas of activity have been introduced to the schools by interested school personnel who maintained a curiosity about the new development and thought it could be useful in improving either his job or the school.

The introduction of extrinsically created ideas and activities usually follows a three-stage process:

1. The administrator, supervisor or teacher who is responsible for the innovation has usually learned of the new idea from a variety of sources such as:

a. Visitations to a school.
b. Attendance at a conference, workshop, lecture, seminar or in a classroom.
c. Consultation with a colleague, expert or instructor.
d. Read about it in a newspaper, magazine or book.

2. With a layman's knowledge of the innovation, the educator may wish to study the innovation by further reviewing the literature and systematically studying the validity and feasibility of the new idea. It is at this moment that the person studying and evaluating the inno-

vation must consider the following in order to determine how feasible it would be to implement the innovation in the school:

- Will the innovation solve a problem and raise the performance level of the school personnel and students?
- Is the cost prohibitive?
- Will the innovation create more problems than it will solve?
- Will the board of education, administrators, teachers and parents accept the change?
- Will there be adverse side effects if this innovation is implemented?
- How can support be gained for this innovation?
- What means will be used to communicate important details about the innovation to the school and the community?
- Will the innovations be compatible with the school system educational objectives?

3. A school district may implement the innovation on a pilot basis or a trial basis in order to be able to more effectively manage any problems which may occur during the initial stages of implementation.

If an innovation idea is to be implemented within an entire school district, the need for a comprehensive feasibility study becomes extremely important and very necessary.

The environment in which the innovation is going to be implemented becomes increasingly important with the magnitude of the new idea or activities. Risk increases with magnitude and job survival becomes acutely jeopardized.

TIME INTERVALS FOR SPECIFYING INNOVATIVE OBJECTIVES

Professional skill objectives and personal development objectives are usually developed for achievement within a time period of one year. This is not necessarily true in the case of innovative objectives. Improving the status quo may vary from one year to ten years.

Innovative objectives may be grouped according to whether they are valid for the short haul or the long pull.

The relationship between a long range goal and short range innovative objectives, the latter being controlled by the periodic review of performance, is illustrated in Figure 6-1. The long range goal illustrated is for a three-year period. However, any period of time beyond three

LONG RANGE OBJECTIVES (3 YEAR PERIOD)

School Year	1971 – 72	1972 – 73	1973 – 74
1st Quarter Review	Short Range Objective Developed	Short Range Objective Modified	
2nd Quarter Review	Short Range Objective Modified		
3rd Quarter Review	Short Range Objective Continued as is		
4th Quarter Review & Results	Short Range Objective Achieved by Above Plans		

SHORT

RANGE

OBJECTIVE

(1 YEAR PERIOD)

Figure 6-1 THE RELATIONSHIP BETWEEN LONG RANGE GOALS AND SHORT RANGE OBJECTIVES

years can be chosen. The relationship between the long-range goal and the short-range objectives for the first year of the five-year plan is explained as follows:

1. The board of education after reviewing the assessment report, discusses it with the chief school officer and mutually agrees upon long range goals to be achieved over a specified period of time.
2. The long range goals are transmitted to key staff members and each building principal.
3. Staff members and building principals will discuss long range

goals with their staff. Each team and department set first year short range objectives for progressing to and reaching the long range goals.

4 . Each quarter the short range objective may be changed, revised, deleted or modified for the purpose of maintaining a steady course for reaching the long range goals.

To illustrate the relationship between long range goal and short range innovative objectives, the following is a true account of a school district located in Long Island, N.Y., which adopted the concept of school management by objectives and had excellent results in progressing toward a long range goal:

Assessment Report (Partial content)

Strength: Ability of students to perform and achieve average and above average scores on weekly tests given in the daily math classes.

Weakness: Poor performance and very low achievement scores on the regents' examinations.

Need: To increase significantly, the percentage of students passing the math regents' examination.

The board of education established that increasing the number of students passing the math regents would be one of the priority long range goals for the school year 1970-71.

After a discussion by the board of education concerning the weakness stated in the Needs Assessment Report, the chief school officer developed the following long range goal:

Long Range Goal:

To raise the percentage of students in the high school passing the math regents' examination from 10% to 80% by June, 1974. (4 years)

The long range goal was reviewed with the board of education and it was mutually agreed that the time span for the achievement of the goal should be reduced by one year; therefore, the long range goal became a three-year plan instead of four. The modified long range plan was disseminated to all staff members and was published in the monthly newsletter circulated to community members.

The central administration staff (3 members) and the secondary high school principal discussed the long range goals. The principal was asked to discuss the long range goals with his staff and draft his proposal in terms of short range objectives and an action plan for reaching the long range goals. The draft was reviewed by the central administration staff and mutually agreed upon by all parties. The first year short range objective was as follows:

Short Range Objective:

   In collaboration with the director of curriculum, the math department chairman and members of the math department, we will use prior regents' tests to determine common weaknesses of students. The findings will be used to develop a remedial math workshop to assure the passing of 25% of the students taking regents' examinations by June, 1971.

Action Plan:

1 . Meet with director of curriculum, math department chairman and math teachers to discuss what can be done to raise the performance levels on regents' examinations. (September 1, 1970)
2 . Develop a course outline to be used in the math workshop sessions for students. (September 3, 1970)
3 . Design simulated regents' test periods for the purpose of observing the number of students who have psychological withdrawals resulting from fear of exams. (September 3, 1970)
4 . Develop math workshops for teachers to discuss effective methods and techniques used in teaching math problems. (September 6, 1970)
5 . Have students with past performance scores take the regents' in January, 1971 to compare the past with the present scores for the purpose of assessing individual achievements as a result of attending the remedial math workshops.
6 . The percentage of students passing the January, 1971 regents' will serve as a guide to determine necessary steps to be taken to ascertain that 25% of all students taking the June, 1971 regents' in math will pass.

The first periodic review report on the short range objective revealed that the objective would be reached as planned.

The second periodic review report on the short range objective indicated that 20% of the students passed the January, 1971 math regents'. The following action plans were mutually agreed to by the high school principal and the math teachers, if the short range objective was to be reached:

   a. Administer a minimum of two simulated math regents' tests per week to all students who will take the math regents'.
   b. Select those students who need a minimum of assistance in terms of one-to-one tutoring and provide them with a special after school program. (February 1, 1971)

The third periodic review report on the short range objective revealed that the objective was expected to be achieved above plans.

The fourth and final periodic review of performance for the first year short range objective indicated that 39% of the students passed the regents' tests in June, 1971. This information was submitted to the board of education by the chief school officer.

In August, 1971, the high school principal modified the minimum standard of the first short range objective to read, ". . . to assure the passing by 65% of the students taking the mathematics regents' examination by June, 1972" and established the revised version of the first year short range objectives as his short range objective for the second year.

IMPORTANT RULES TO CONSIDER WHEN INTRODUCING CHANGE IN A SCHOOL

The feasibility of introducing an innovation into a school system usually will be based upon how successfully the educational leaders can foresee the implementation problems and how effectively they work with school personnel and the community. It is important for the administrator to give serious consideration to the following:

1. Some teachers are reluctant to implement a change if it originates from administrators. The most effective method to effect change is to let the need and the plans for the change emanate from the teachers themselves.

2. Change will be more acceptable if it is incorporated into a familiar plan or pattern.

3. Change is more likely to occur if there is involvement by the persons most directly affected by the change.

4. Change is multi-dimensional. It may result in changing the individual being affected by the change or the change may involve the situation—changing the person's perception of the change.

5. Change may be effected more easily if it emanates from an emergency situation or a dire need.

6. Change should be implemented on a small scale initially so that careful analysis of the effects of the change can be realized which may necessitate creative action hithertofore not realized.

7. Change occurs when the people most affected by the change feel that they are "calling the shots."

8. Change cannot be accomplished by an edict. Educators will achieve change if they can attain their personal goals when attaining the school objectives.

SOME ERRORS TO AVOID WHEN DEVELOPING INNOVATIVE OBJECTIVES

The following is a list of errors which administrators, supervisors and teachers must be careful to avoid when developing innovative objectives in a program of school management by objectives:

1. Objectives are set too low to challenge the person achieving them.

2. Prior results and present conditions are not used as the basis for developing intrinsically-oriented creative objectives.

3. Common objectives are neither stated nor clarified.

4. Common objectives of the individual department are not meshed with the school's objectives.

5. Individual persons are overloaded with inappropriate or impossible objectives.

6. Designating two persons to be responsible for doing the same task when it would be better to designate the responsibility to one person.

7. Stressing method for achieving results rather than clarifying individual responsibility.

8. Making no administrative policy or procedure as a basis for performing but waiting for results.

9. Tacitly emphasizing that what pleases "me" is more important than achieving the stated objective.

10. Successful performance of behavior is not reinforced with compliments, rewards, awards etc., and unsuccessful performance or behavior goes unattended without reprimands, written reports etc.

11. Failure to permit the introduction of new ideas and activities from outside the school district or discouraging school personnel from doing so, thereby making very little attempt to improve the school.

12. Failure to establish periodical assessment data to measure progress of objectives.

13. Failure to discontinue innovative practices which have failed to produce results or are unfeasible or impossible to achieve.

14. Failure on the part of the administrator to think through and act on the assistance he must give teachers to aid on the achievement of their objectives.

15. Ignoring the real issues or obstacles that are inclined to hinder the achievement of innovative objectives such as problem-solving objectives and professional skill objectives which consume a great deal of time.

16. Ignoring innovative objectives proposed by teachers.

17. Failure to cluster areas of responsiblilities in the most appropriate job.

18. Failure to determine what program has been proposed to achieve the objectives and/or accepting all objectives without a plan for successful achievement.

It is extremely important for those who are developing innovative objectives to examine the past results or present conditions as a basis for ascertaining ideas and points of departure for developing new innovative objectives for the coming school year or modifying those objectives which were created unrealistically. However, the reader must be careful that he is not fooled by common errors because of his grouping of facts or because breakdowns and analyses of data were not accomplished in a systematic and logical manner. In an effort to put educators "on guard" to avoid these common errors the following is suggested:

1. Beware of the Bias Effect

An educator may have a particular bias or a deep desire to achieve the innovative objectives of the school and in so doing may cause the educator to produce evidence that demonstrates what they want to occur and not necessarily what has actually taken place. This positive attitude about the innovation is known as the Hawthorne Effect. This phenomenon persists with most creative activities or ideas for a short period of time and usually diminishes with time and/or experience. The nongraded concept was one extrinsic innovation which helped to produce this effect. In order to be a part of what a good idea seemed to be, many administrators in the late 1960's maintained that they had implemented the nongraded concept. What usually occurred was a glorified traditional program.

2. Don't expect Too Much Too Soon

Most innovative objectives will take time to be felt. Improvement for the first year may only account for a small increase in performance. This is to be expected. Ancient methods and techniques will need to give way to new ideas and activities. Old wounds will need time to heal. However, after a sufficient period of time, the change desired should have been realized or there may be a need to revert to those "ancient times".

3. Don't base Decisions on Insufficient Sampling

Quite often in public schools a pilot project is implemented before efforts are made to introduce a program on a large scale. If the pilot project is a miniature duplication of the larger effort, so much the better; however, in the past this has not always been the case. Either the pilot project was not large enough to reveal all the problems generated when implementing the innovation or erroneous information was obtained from the pilot project which led to false assumptions about the innovation. Even pilot projects that are large enough may not necessarily produce actual results or conditions for implementing the creative idea.

ADMINISTRATOR'S ROLE IN DEVELOPING INNOVATIVE OBJECTIVES

It is the task of administrators to induce teachers to set innovative objectives to achieve their goals. During the conference session, the administrator should ask specific questions that will require the educator to reflect and to develop new methods and techniques to deal with existing problems. The administrator may be able to generate creative ideas and activities from the educator by getting him to seriously consider the following essential data:

1. Have the facts of the situation been thoroughly examined in order to direct attention in those critical areas needing improvement? For example, if the situation needing improvement is in the area of reading, critical questions are: Why are the students not achieving? Is it due to the fault of the program? . . . the students? . . . the teachers?

2. Can the facts be organized into some logical order? It may become obvious that the students are able to read because the teachers are not proficient in teaching reading and then the next item becomes apparent.

3. Now that cause and effect have been identified, the next step involves the administrator coaching the teacher to generate alternatives for solving the reading problem. Here the alternative may be to bring in a reading specialist to assist teachers with the reading program or to conduct an in-service reading course.

4. Once the alternatives have been exposed, the next step involves the selection of the best alternative to solve the problem, after which,

5. The teacher then develops the innovative objective which is mutually agreed to by all parties.

Setting innovative objectives is important to the improvement of the schools and sometimes to the survival of the chief school officer. Every educator is a manager of the school and therefore is expected continuously to set innovative objectives for improving the school.

SUMMARY

Innovative objectives are the highest order of objectives. They are innovation-oriented objectives which are set to improve the status quo. The right to expect all school personnel to set innovative objectives has four corollaries:

1. The school person who does not set any innovative objectives should receive no special considerations.
2. The school person who fails to achieve professional skill objectives should be replaced or fired.

3 . Failure to achieve innovative objectives should not be as severe a penalty as failure to achieve professional skill objectives.
4 . The school person who constantly tries to improve performance by innovative objectives should be encouraged and supported.

Developing innovative objectives usually falls into two categories: Intrinsic innovative objectives which involve the introduction of new ideas, methods, systems, techniques from the inside, and extrinsic innovative objectives which describe a new idea or activity which was introduced from a source outside of the school to improve the performance of the school.

The time interval applicable to innovative objectives falls into two major categories:

1 . Short range objectives are those to be completed within a one year period.
2 . Long range goals are those with a completion date of three years or more.

The feasibility of introducing innovations into the school will depend to a large extent on how successful the educational leaders are in foreseeing problems. Some errors to avoid when developing innovative objectives are: (1) overlooking the bias effect; (2) expecting too much too soon; (3) basing decisions on insufficient samplings.

SEVEN

Formulating Personal Development Objectives

Many schools across the nation are attempting to make sweeping improvements. Don E. Clines states:

> The seeds of dissatisfaction with present efforts are being sown in the basis of a strong conviction that something better must be created for the future . . . The great problem is to replace the obsolete programs, procedures, and buildings currently in use with a dramatically new concept in education.[1]

The job of retraining educators is a herculean task, but not impossible. Teachers can't change easily. The responsibility for professional growth is a joint responsibility of the school district and the educators. The school district must provide the time, resources and opportunities to re-evaluate and retrain the school personnel. Likewise the teacher must also provide the time, expense and opportunities for personal development. In an objective-centered performance appraisal program the teacher's personal development efforts are delineated in clearly defined statements of objectives which were mutually agreed to by the administrator. Thus, by retraining, a teacher becomes an integral part of the operations of the school. In this chapter, the reader will be presented with a definition of personal development objectives, an elaboration of personal development (everybody's responsibility), information on guiding educators for setting personal development

---

[1] Edgar L. Morphet and Charles O. Ryan, *Designing Education for the Future, No. 3*, Citation Press, New York, 1967. "Don E. Clines Planning and Effecting Needed Changes in Individual Schools," p. 163.

objectives, consideration areas in personal development and personal development activities.

DEFINING PERSONAL DEVELOPMENT OBJECTIVES

Personal development objectives are aimed at improving the personal skills of school personnel in order that they may perform their tasks in a less perfunctory manner. This kind of development may take place as a result of directed experience on the job or via formal classes in teaching skills or technical and professional subjects. All major forms of objectives are a form of personal development. The fact that they may be job-centered does not exclude them from personally improving the school personnel.

PERSONAL DEVELOPMENT—EVERYBODY'S RESPONSIBILITY

Since educators are assigned to carry out the goals of the school, change can only be affected by change in the manner in which they perform. At times, there is almost total reliance placed on the personal development of the staff for producing change. The importance of a strong personal development program through the process of school management by objectives for the promotion of institutional change can hardly be overemphasized.

All organizational change and all innovative objectives depend to some extent on the willingness and the activity of educators to change or to improve their ways of performing on the job. In institutions such as a school district, the human element is extremely important if not the most important factor.

Whether change is induced through the authority-controlled relationship or whether it is done through the participating decision-making process may greatly affect the genuine acceptance with which educators proceed to change, thereby affecting the quality of the change outcome. Another important factor which may affect the quality of the change outcome is whether educators have had the opportunity to acquire the necessary knowledge, skill, and related attitudes and values setting their own personal development objectives for improving themselves professionally. School management by objectives lends itself to this type of program and, if implemented correctly, it can affect both the ability and willingness of educators to change. The school district is an institution where the school staff tends to aspire to professional autonomy and status. When such is the case, personal development becomes everybody's responsibility. Educators will feel responsibility for developing personal development objectives to meet their own individual needs.

GUIDING EDUCATORS FOR SETTING PERSONAL DEVELOPMENT OBJECTIVES

Personal development objectives and, to some extent, professional skills and innovative objectives are designed to change or modify the behavior of educators. Changing the behavior of educators in significant ways is a complex leadership responsibility involving many problems for the administration. All objectives must be set for their genuine significance to the operation of the school district. Staff members must be guided and stimulated toward objective attainment. The selection of personal development objectives by both teachers and administrators requires careful planning. The use of innovative objectives, selected activities which posed problems in the past, and the performance appraisal report should provide substantial basis for the development of personal development objectives.

Personal development activities and programs for generating optimum effectiveness from educators must be designed with an understanding of the kind of behavioral change that can genuinely be expected to occur. Administrators cannot continue to expect changes in the teachers by presenting a cafeteria assortment of in-service education courses and courses taken at higher educational institutions. These programs may be ineffective or even produce undesired results.

If personal development objectives are to serve a function, the following points should be observed:

1 . There should be a mutually-agreed-upon reason for performing the activities.
2 . The total effect of the changes in the behavior of the person performing the activity should be evaluated in terms of their importance to the goals of the program.
3 . The personal development objective should be included as a part of the Statement of Performance Objectives.
4 . There should be follow-up on the progress of the personal development activities.

Personal development objectives provide opportunities for the staff to think through situations and arrive at problems through self-development activities themselves.

The relationship or interlocking aspect of an innovative objective and a personal development objective is illustrated in Figure 7-1. An explanation follows:

- An educator gets an idea about an innovation for producing change to get improved results. It is discussed with his immediate supervisor and it is mutually agreed to implement the change.
- The educator develops the idea into long range goal and short range innovative objective and action plan.
- The educator also develops a short range personal development objective for the development and training of the staff for implementing the innovation. The objective is mutually agreed to by all parties concerned.
- The training and development program is initiated to change and/or modify the behavior of the staff to affect the change.
- The idea is implemented.
- Results are evaluated through periodic and quarterly review of of performance (change).
- Comparison is made between the perception of the idea and the actual results.

The following is an innovative objective (short range) which was developed by a principal and mentioned in a previous chapter.

Short Range Objective (Innovative)

Utilizing the service of Mr. George Cureton, Reading Consultant for the school district, I (principal) will implement the Cureton Reading Program in my building during the school year 1971-72 and increase the percentage of students on grade level in reading from 23 per cent to 50 per cent, as measured by the Metropolitan Achievement Test.

Using the above short range objective as a base or guide, the principal developed the following personal development objective and action plan.

Short Range Objective (Personal Development)

Retaining the services of Mr. George Cureton for the months of July and August, I (principal) will implement a workshop

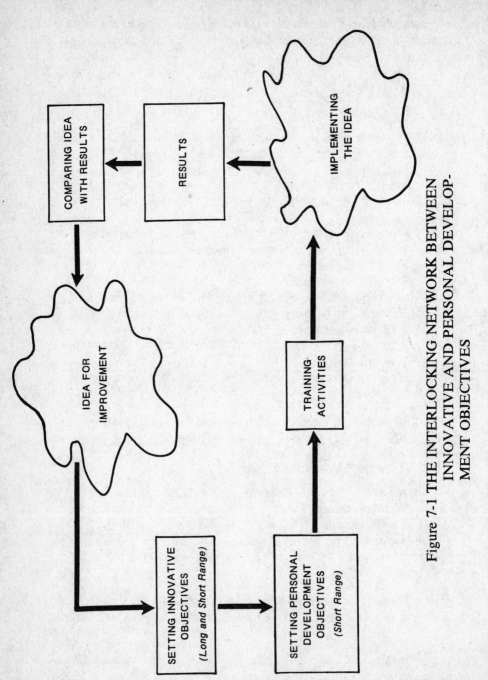

Figure 7-1 THE INTERLOCKING NETWORK BETWEEN INNOVATIVE AND PERSONAL DEVELOP-MENT OBJECTIVES

on the Cureton Reading Program. I will strive for a 90% attendance of the teachers in my building.

Action Plans

1. Assisted by the federal aid coordinator, director of curriculum and instruction, and Mr. George Cureton, develop a proposal using State Education guidelines. Target date: February 27, 1971.
2. Obtain approval from the ESEA, Title I Office at State Education Department. Target date: April 15, 1971.
3. Obtain results on the three experimental classes presently implementing the Cureton Reading Program and disseminate to staff for discussion. Target date: May 1, 1971.
4. Distribute information on workshop on Cureton Reading Program and request members to sign up to enroll in either the July or August workshop. Target date: May 10, 1971.
5. Personally contact those teachers not enrolling in the summer workshop and get them to attend. Target date: May 15, 1971.
6. Assisted by Mr. Cureton, Director of Curriculum and Instruction, we will develop all of the necessary instructional tools and materials for the Workshop. Target date: July 5, 1971.
7. Implement the July workshop and evaluate on a weekly basis. Revise and strengthen the workshop as needed. Target date: July 5, 1971.
8. Develop a questionnaire to get the reaction of the staff about the value of the Cureton reading workshop. Target Date: July 10, 1971.
9. Implement the August workshop making necessary changes as indicated in the July workshop. Target date: August 1, 1971.
10. Assist federal aid coordinator in completing the evaluation portion of the ESEA Title I reporting forms. Target date: August 1, 1971.

CONSIDERATION AREAS IN PERSONAL DEVELOPMENT

Personal development objectives are specified for the purpose of projecting an annual program for professional growth and development. Such a program when well-planned and organized is not only valuable in improving the competency of the professional staff but also aids in the improvement of the school district. When personal development objectives are being considered, the following areas should be recognized:

1. Effective school management techniques.
2. Improved techniques and methods of teaching, supervision and administration.
3. Improved knowledge in areas of concentration.
4. Better insight into the dynamics of teaching and learning.
5. The changing role of the educator.
6. Better insight into one's self.
7. Better understanding of students.
8. Better human relations.
9. Effective strategies for teaching.

PERSONAL DEVELOPMENT ACTIVITIES

The following is a list of professional growth activities which may be included in the personal development section of the Statement of Performance Objectives.

1. Visits to Exemplary Schools

These visitations may be initiated by the teacher, supervisor or administrator and are usually to observe a program, method, technique or practice of interest to the educator which may benefit the school district. These visits may occur within or outside of the school district.

2. Sabbatical Leaves

A leave of absence for personal development and growth often takes the form of a sabbatical leave at the end of a period of time, usually of seven years' service. Sabbatical leave may be granted for travel, study or research. Some school districts continue a portion of the teacher's salary during the sabbatical leave; some school districts pay all or part of the tuition at a college or university of the educator's choice, whether the educator is on leave or during the school year.

3. Attendance at Board Meetings

Sometimes educators may gain some insight into the complexities of operating a school which can be of some value to them professionally.

4. Relevant Work Experience

Usually this work experience is gained through summer employment. For example, a biology teacher may be able to obtain employment in a hospital.

Even if the work experience is not directly related to the education area of specialty, valuable experience may be gained by better understanding of people.

5. Attendance at Professional Performances, Workshops, Seminars and Lectures

Many schools across the country are encouraging and making it possible for educators to attend and participate in conferences, workshops, seminars, lectures and encounter groups.

6. Writing Assignments

Much can be learned from various writing assignments. Writing a professional manuscript; researching and publishing a scholarly professional article; writing and following through on a federal or state project; understanding and reporting on a special study within the school district, and preparing special reports and speeches for supervisors are all worthwhile experiences.

7. Community Affairs

Participation in community meetings, activities, and programs is an excellent source for personal development.

8. Reading Program

Personal growth can be acquired from a reading program which involves a specific number of books in an area of concentration. By subscribing to various educationally-oriented literature, establishing small professional reading clubs within the school, reading for isolating information, developing a bibliography in a special subject area and setting up a professional library section in the school district, this area of growth can be sustained.

9. Job Rotation

Educators have been known to improve themselves professionally by participation in a number of job-rotating activities. These include substitution for teachers, supervisors and administrators, rotating to a position in another school and special research and development assignments. Educators can find unusual opportunities for personal development by teaching in a neighboring school district, another state or abroad.

10. Course Work

An assortment of professional courses conducted in a local college or university, an in-service course (a career development course) held within the school or sponsored by regional associations are valuable sources for professional growth.

11. Professional Services

Educators grow professionally when they extend their services in a variety of activities, such as service as a consultant in another school district, participating in planning a project, or being a guest speaker at a university class, conference, etc.

12. Travel

Teachers and administrators have been known to improve themselves professionally by traveling within the United States and/or to foreign countries. Each year the federal government provides opportunities for numerous educators to visit certain foreign countries, all expenses paid. These visits usually take place to study the country and/or to observe the schools.[2]

[2] George B. Brain and Thomas C. Pullen, Jr., *Increasing Your Administrative Skills in Dealing with the Instructional Program*. Prentice-Hall, Inc., Englewood Cliffs, N.J., 1966, pp. 38-45.

Using the above resource information about personal development objectives, they may appear as the following:

> Given an opportunity to spend a minimum of two hours daily, for a period of one week, in training with John Klein working on Individual Study Units, I will, during that period of time, complete a minimum of five (5) individual study units which will be tried in a class and be acceptable for further use, as determined by a four member team of teachers.

> I will attend Teachers College, Columbia University during the Fall semester, 1970 and work toward the completion of the requirements for the Ed.D. by performing the following:

> 1 . Undertaking field work (at Wyandanch Memorial Senior High School), October, 1970-February, 1971.
> 2 . Take a minimum of sixteen hours of academic work during the fall and spring semesters.

> Given appropriate training and experience of not less than three (3) hours per day for one (1) week in the independent study center for English under the direction of the teacher-in-charge at the Wyandanch High School, I will conduct classes utilizing Individual Study Units, with those students assigned for remedial work to the satisfaction of the teacher-in-charge and the high school principal.

Usually personal development objectives will only account for a small portion of the Statement of Performance Objectives. School personnel should probably limit themselves to three to five self-development objectives per school year. However, if the school personnel are trainees, there may be as much as 25 to 50 per cent of the Statements of Performance Objectives geared to personal development activities.

A superintendent once stated, "whatever enhances the person, enhances the school." This is the philosophy behind the personal development objectives and should be an integral part of the Statement of Performance Objectives. However, it must be pointed out that school personnel should not spend an inordinate amount of time and energy with personal development activities to the extent that other objectives are not being met. This will surely impair performance.

Most school districts noted for their innovations have elaborate programs for nurturing the professional development of their staffs. Innovative objectives reinforce the need for personal development opportunity. No school can be improved without both.

SUMMARY

Personal development objectives are aimed directly at improving the personal skills of school personnel in order to perform their tasks in a more efficient manner.

Educators should use the innovative objectives as the base for setting personal development objectives. The interlocking network between innovative and personal development objectives are: An educator gets an idea—the educator develops the idea into long range goals and short range innovative objectives—the educator develops a short range personal development objective—the training and development program is initiated—the idea is implemented—results are evaluated—personal development is everybody's responsibility—staff members must be guided and stimulated toward objective attainment.

Personal development objectives are specified for the purpose of projecting an annual program for the professional growth and development of school personnel. The list of personal development activities include: visitation to exemplary schools, sabbatical leaves, attendance at board meetings, work experience, attendance at professional conferences, workshops, seminars and lectures, writing assignments, reading programs, job rotation, course work and professional services.

EIGHT

Administering the Performance Appraisal Program

The administration of the school management by objectives' approach should be made as simple as possible consistent with maximum effectiveness. This means that someone in top authority must have responsibility for the administration of the program. It means that operational procedures for setting objectives must be established. It means that the objectives must be recorded in standardized format. It means that the reporting makes the degree of variation in performance easily discernible. It means that the form for reporting results must provide for monitoring performance and for improving the opportunity for achieving objectives. It means that a form should be devised for guiding and directing the administrator in conducting the conference. It also means that the reports must be maintained in a manner that permits immediate checks to be made concerning performance. The rationale for the chapter is to elaborate on all of these items.

ADMINISTRATIVE RESPONSIBILITY

The responsibility for the implementation of school management by objectives and the objective-centered approach to performance appraisal should rest with the superintendent or an assistant superintendent. This administrator should have the authority to direct and/or to correct the necessary action for the successful installation of the program in the school system.

In a large school system, the responsibility for the administrative aspects of the program is frequently delegated to another top administrator. To a large extent this can be controlled by the way in which the program is being implemented. For example, if school management by objectives is implemented solely for appraisal purposes, the assistant superintendent for personnel would be the most likely person to perform the administrative task. However, if the program is to be implemented for multiple uses, such as organizing, planning and controlling activities of the school system, an administrator who has had some measure of experience with planning and school management by objectives should be retained by the school system to assume complete charge of the program. Dr. Marcus Foster, Superintendent of Schools in Oakland, California, and one of the pioneering school administrators who has been successfully implementing school management by objectives in his school system, has hired several administrators to assume the responsibility of administering the program. These administrative positions are: Associate Superintendent for Planning, Research and Evaluation; Assistant for Captial Planning and PPBS and Special Assistant for Management Training.

ESTABLISHING OPERATIONAL PROCEDURES
FOR SETTING OBJECTIVES

When the concept of school management by objectives is implemented in the school system, every attempt must be made to eliminate confusion concerning who reports to whom and what procedures are taken to mediate an impasse between a teacher and his immediate supervisor. The most effective method to deal with this problem is by establishing operational procedures for setting objectives. Once the procedures are in the hands of each professional staff member, a special meeting can be held by the building principal to discuss and to clear up any questions. The operational procedures for setting objectives should include Reporting Instructions and Mediation Instructions.

REPORTING INSTRUCTIONS

Usually the educator's immediate supervisor is the person responsible for initiating the quarterly (every ten weeks) post appraisal conferences. However, there are situations in which more than one person is responsible for initiating the post appraisal conference. The following is how the reporting procedure is established for a medium size school district. The point of the symbol ($\angle$) indicates the responsibility for the conference for directing and guiding the setting of objectives and the performance review.

CENTRAL ADMINISTRATIVE STAFF

Board of Education	$\angle$ Superintendent
Superintendent	$\angle$ Assistant Superintendent
	Administration
	Finance
	Instruction
	Personnel
	Federal Aid Coordinator
Assistant Superintendents	
Administration	$\angle$ Directors
	Transportation
	Cafeteria
	Maintenance & Grounds
Finance	$\angle$ Chief Payroll Clerk
Instruction	$\angle$ Director of Secondary Education
	Secondary Principal
	Director of Elementary Education
	Elementary Principal
Personnel	$\angle$ Director of Pupil Personnel
	Secondary Principal
	Elementary Principal
Director of Pupil Personnel	$\angle$ Director of Guidance
	Director of Psychological Services
	Social Worker
	Attendance Teacher

SECONDARY SCHOOLS

Secondary Principal	$\angle$ Assistant Principals
Assistant Principal	$\angle$ Department Chairmen
	English
	Mathematics

Social Studies
Science
Physical Education
Special Areas

Department Chairmen   ∠ Area Teachers

ELEMENTARY SCHOOLS

Elementary Principal   ∠ Assistant Principals
Assistant Principal   ∠ Team Leaders (5 Teams)
Team Leaders   ∠ Teachers

In most cases there is a one-to-one relationship for setting objectives and goal attainment. However, in order to accommodate the overlapping responsibility of some roles, several positions will need to confer on common goals. Therefore, it may become necessary to set up "trio" formation or "quartet" formation for conferring on goals. Such is the case of the Director of Secondary Education and Secondary Principal reporting to the Assistant Superintendent for Instruction.

MEDIATING CONFLICTS

If a conflict should exist between two or more persons during a conference on setting goals or performance review, the supervisor should be contacted to help reach a mutual agreement. However, if the disagreement concerns curriculum and instruction, the assistant superintendent of instruction should be contacted to mediate. If the disagreement concerns personnel, then the assistant superintendent of personnel should be contacted to help solve the problem. If all efforts fail, then the superintendent should be called in to help arrive at a mutual agreement by the two parties involved; then, if he fails, he renders a decision that stands for both parties.

RECORDING OBJECTIVES

One important aspect of the objective-centered approach to performance appraisal is that once there is a mutual agreement on performance objectives by the administrator and teacher they should be recorded in writing. The reason for this is simple. Mental goals are subject to change more rapidly than recorded goals. As human beings, we tend to change goals depending upon our experience in meeting our goals. We tend to remember those things that turn out the way we want or see them and tend to modify or forget those things that turn out less than we desire. When goals are recorded in writing, we can neither forget or deny them. Recorded goals serve as a guide to keep teachers on track for fulfilling their professional obligations. Recorded goals are positive and tangible evidence for a course of action. Recorded goals serve as checks on performance. Recorded goals serve as a means by which teachers are provided assistance, counseling and recommendations by the administrator for improving performance. Recorded goals serve as a reliable guide for evaluating the effectiveness of administrators.

CONSTRUCTING THE STATEMENT OF PERFORMANCE OBJECTIVES

The Statement of Performance Objectives is the instrument used to record performance objectives and action plan to be followed in the execution of a teacher or administrator's professional responsibility. It states the conditions that will exist when the objectives are satisfactorily achieved. The following is a list of component parts of the Statement of Performance Objectives:

1. The Title, usually appearing at the top of the statement, must specify the description of the statement, the name of the teacher or administrator submitting the statement, and the school year for which the statement is intended.
2. The Position, usually appearing below and left of the title of the statement, describes the professional position of the educator setting the objectives.
3. The School, appearing with the address, is located immediately following the position.
4. Performance Objectives, appearing below the school and location. Professional Skills, Problem-Solving, Innovative and Personal Development Objectives with Action Plans are listed as indicated.
5. Acceptance Statement, appears with date after the last objective and action plan. The statement must be signed by the teacher or administrator and his immediate supervisor. Date should also appear with the signatures.

The Statement of Performance Objectives is completed in three copies. The original remains with the educator, one copy is submitted to the immediate supervisor and the remaining copy is forwarded to the chief school officer.

ADVANTAGES OF THE STATEMENT OF PERFORMANCE OBJECTIVES

The Statement of Performance Objectives has several advantages:

1. Every teacher and administrator wants to know how he stands with his immediate supervisor. The Statement of Performance Objectives is the basis upon which educators are evaluated.

2. The Statement of Performance Objectives directs each and every professional employee's attention to all aspects of the job. Because of the individuality which exists in the educational environment, each educator should be evaluated individually in order to minimize the possibility of overlooking essential and vital elements of success and for the successful achievement of individual objectives. The Statement of Performance Objectives provides us with the instrument for assessing individual performances.

3. Recorded objectives built into a statement which has been mutually agreed to establish a firm foundation for objective evaluation of the performance of teacher and administrator.

4. The Statement of Performance Objectives not only serves as a useful appraisal device for the administrator but it also serves as a useful guide for the administrator to appraise his own performance. When educators begin assessing their own performance in terms of the achievement of their goals, we have a form of multiple self-initiated evaluation which is desirable and needed in most schools.

5. The Statement of Performance Objectives may also serve as an aid in the development and growth of the school personnel. Performance objectives are closely interwoven with staff development and growth.

6. The statement which describes the performance objectives is a document which helps to improve on-the-job personnel relationships. When an educator knows what his objectives are and what actions are needed for achieving the objectives, his attitude will improve his relationship to his job.

7. The Statement of Performance Objectives is a "guide" which

helps educators to think in terms of specific performance objectives and how to achieve them. As a result, both individual and overall performances are performed.

DISADVANTAGES OF THE STATEMENT OF PERFORMANCE OBJECTIVES

It would be less than honest to delineate the advantages of the Statement of Performance Objectives without indicating some of the possible disadvantages.

1. The Statement of Performance Objectives does not guarantee adequate performance. A teacher or an administrator can make himself look good if he can get his immediate supervisor to mutually agree to objectives which can be achieved without much effort.

2. The Statement of Performance Objectives is not a cure-all for unscrupulous educators. A well-developed statement can be used as a basis for parlaying mediocre performance into an outstanding performance appraisal rating.

3. Unless the teacher or administrator is required to substantiate on plan or above plan performance by providing supportive documents, the Statement of Performance Objectives can be used as a tool to help cover up below plan performance.

Following is an example of a Statement of Performance Objectives.

STATEMENT OF PERFORMANCE OBJECTIVES MRS. MARY WILKERSON SCHOOL YEAR 1972-73

Position: Elementary Teacher
School: Milton L. Olive Elementary School
          Wyandanch, New York

Professional Skill Objectives

1 .1—*Short Range Objective:*

> During the third period for the next four weeks, I will visit the classrooms of several exemplary teachers so that I can observe their teaching styles and learn how they maintain classroom conduct. The success of this objective will be determined by a satisfactory rating from the principal.

Action Plan:

1. Request the principal to submit the names of six exemplary teachers by September 18, 1972.
2. Discuss my plan with each exemplary teacher, and arrange to visit their individual classrooms by September 24, 1972.
3. Visit classroom as planned.
4. Describe and discuss various techniques used by each teacher, not more than one day after each visitation.
5. Assimilate what I learned.

1.2—*Short Range Objective:*

Assisted by the curriculum associate, I will develop a series of reading tapes and work sheets to reinforce skills in decoding, already taught. The success of this objective will be determined by a 25% increase in students' performance in decoding skills after the materials have been in use for a period of four months.

Action Plan:

1. Become thoroughly familiar with the school district reading guide by September 20, 1972.
2. Meet with the curriculum associate to discuss plans for developing reading tapes and work sheets, and to obtain his cooperation by September 22, 1972.
3. Obtain six blank tapes from media specialist by September 23, 1972.
4. Meet with the curriculum associate and discuss procedural steps for developing reading tapes and work sheets. Mutually agree to a schedule whereby both of us can meet to develop these materials by October 3, 1972.
5. Present first draft of written materials to principal for his suggestions by November 1, 1972.
6. Make necessary adjustments and present to clerk-typist for typing by November 4, 1972.
7. Implement reading tape series and worksheets into the reading program by November 15, 1972.

1.3—*Short Range Objective:*

Using a taped lesson as a guide, I will improve my questioning techniques with my class by:

a. Asking the question first, then calling on the student to answer.

2. Use the student's response to a question as a springboard for dialogue among the rest of the class.

c. Use a maximum of two sentences to elicit responses from the students.

d. Keep my dialogue to a maximum of twenty-five per cent.

The success of this objective is determined by a satisfactory rating from the principal.

Action Plan:

1. Meet with the principal and request him to arrange for media aid to tape one of my lessons by September 17, 1972.

2. Using this tape as a guide, determine my present questioning status, types of questions presently being asked in class, and the frequency of each type of question asked. Identify needs in questioning techniques by discussing my findings with the principal and getting his advice by developing a basic criteria guide for asking questions by Sept. 30, 1972.

3. Develop the basic criteria guide by October 5, 1972.

4. Arrange to have the media aid tape another lesson. Compare new tape with old tape and make necessary adjustments by October 15, 1972.

5. Request principal to evaluate lesson for effective questioning techniques by October 30, 1972.

1.4—*Short Range Objective:*

Given a student or class problem, I will use the problem-solving conference as a technique for problem solving. A minimum of 75% of the students must give a satisfactory rating to this technique as determined by a survey.

Action Plan:

1. Identify the problem-solving techniques to the class and get their consent to implement the concept by September 10, 1972.

2. Whenever a problem arises, call the students together, identify the problem, and get the students to provide alternative solutions to the problem.

3. Get the students to reach a consensus over the best solution to the problem.

1 .5—Short Range Objective:

In order to better understand my pupils, I will visit each student's home and confer with his parents. This objective will be successfully achieved if I visit the homes of all of my students.

Action Plan:

1 . Develop a tentative schedule for visiting the homes of my students by October 1, 1972.
2 . Construct an outline of what I will discuss with each parent by October 5, 1972.
3 . Bring along a summary of each student's achievement.
4 . Contact each parent at least three days before the visit. Wear informal clothing. Keep the parent at ease.
5 . Return to the classroom and log the results of each visit, denoting attitude of parents, conditions of house, etc.

Problem-Solving Objectives

Problem:

4th grade teachers are not teaching health education, which is mandated by the New York State Education Dept.

2 .1—Short Range Objective:

Given a health curriculum, fourth grade teachers will teach a minimum of two (2) health lessons a week from November 1, 1972 to June 23, 1973.

1 . Pessimistic Goal: Less than 2 lessons a week should be considered satisfactory.
2 . Realistic Goal: Two health lessons a week is the usual amount of instruction in most schools in other districts and should be expected here.
3 . Optimistic Goal: More than two lessons a week would be considered highly satisfactory.

Action Plan:

1 . Request the State Education Dept. to forward curriculum guide to school district by September 15, 1972.
2 . Distribute to members of team, curriculum guide for their review by September 22, 1972.
3 . Three team members meet after school with director of curriculum and instruction and health coordinator

to discuss New York State Curriculum Guide and legal needs by September 29, 1972.

4. Arrangements be made to excuse team members from classes for a period of two weeks to develop 4th grade curriculum for health education by Oct. 5, 1972.
5. Fourth grade health curriculum is developed by October 19, 1972.
6. Director of curriculum and instruction and health coordinator conduct meeting with all team members to discuss health curriculum by October 20, 1972.
7. Fourth grade health curriculum is evaluated at end of school year for additional content, revisions and omissions.
8. Teach at least two health lessons a week from November 1, 1972 to June 20, 1973.
9. Monitor student progress on profile sheet from November 1, 1972 to June 20, 1973.
10. Confer at least monthly with health coordinator on student profiles.

Innovative Objectives

Long Range Goal:

To reduce the teachers' absentee rate from approximately ten days for teachers per school year to five days for teachers per school year by June 30, 1974 (3 years).

Standards:

1. Total staff involvement.
2. Program adopted must be devised and mutually agreed to by the principal and teaching staff.

3.1—Short Range Objective:

Working as an effective team, we will design a procedure for adjusting to team members' absence in order to reduce the need for substitute teachers. (Minimal level of acceptable standard is determined by the number of substitutes during the present school year which should account for no more than seven per teacher for one team.)

Action Plan:

1. Team meets to discuss the long range goal with the chief school officer by September 25, 1972.

2. Team members meet to determine alternative strategies by September 20, 1972 for achieving objectives.
3. Select best alternative by September 25, 1972 for reaching objectives.
4. Establish and maintain a chart on number of substitute teachers hired each month and check to determine if objectives will be reached if the same rate continues.
5. Make necessary adjustments in order to reach objective.

Long Range Goal:

To raise the number of students in grade 4 on grade level in science from 25% to 85% by June, 1974.

3.2—Short Range Objective:

Given $1500.00 for equipment and materials, assistance from the district curriculum staff to implement a lab-centered 4th grade science course so that a minimum of 60% of the 4th grade students will successfully complete the course.

Standards:

1. At least 95% of the students will complete all the lab units.
2. At least 85% of the students will pass all the unit tests.
3. At least 60% of the students will pass the final 4th grade science achievement test (standardized).

Action Plan:

1. Order needed supplies, etc., by September 25, 1972.
2. Develop detailed course outline and submit to administration by October 10, 1972.
3. Plan and implement 2-3 laboratory-centered lessons (weekly).
4. Develop Student Progress Profile Sheet by October 12, 1972.
5. Prepare daily lessons.
6. Give tests on current topics (weekly).
7. Give unit topic tests (monthly).
8. Take class on trip to following places:
a. Museum of Natural History (by Dec. 15, 1972).
9. To analyze monthly test results and develop supplemental lessons, etc., and adjusted activities for those students showing underachievement.

10. Record student progress, based on weekly tests, on Student Profiles (weekly).
11. Meet with director of curriculum and instruction and curriculum associate to analyze Student Profiles and adjust course plans, etc. (monthly).

Personal Development Objectives

4 .1—*Short Range Objective:*

Given several in-service workshops on the Psychodynamics of Teaching, I will attend a minimum of 90% of these workshops.

Action Plan:

1. Enroll to take the in-service workshop by October 6, 1972.
2. Attend the workshops which are offered every Wednesday in the cafetorium in the Milton L. Olive Elementary School.
3. Apply the principles learned in the workshop in my class on a daily basis.
4. Prepare an article entitled "The Psychodynamics of Teaching a Fourth Grade Class" by Jan. 15, 1973.
5. Distribute the article to the professional staff by January 22, 1973.
6. Submit the article to an educational publisher for publication by February 1, 1973.

4 .2—*Short Range Objective:*

Given two personal business days, I will attend the fourth conference of the National Association for the Individualization of Instruction on November 7-9, 1972; to prepare guidelines for individualizing and humanizing instruction which will be reviewed by the members of my team for use by December 1, 1972.

Action Plan:

1. Fill out registration blank and forward fee by October 15, 1972.
2. Obtain conference program prior to conference and schedule pertinent workshops for individualizing and humanizing instruction.
3. Attend conference (bring along cassette tape recorder and at least 20 cassette cartridges).

4 . Record all pertinent seminars.
5 . Review all seminars which were recorded and jot down helpful information for developing guidelines by November 20, 1972.
6 . Develop outline for guidelines and submit to director of curriculum and instruction and principal for their approval by November 21, 1972.
7 . Develop draft of guidelines by November 25, 1972.
8 . Distribute draft to team for their review and record their suggestions and recommendations by November 28, 1972.
9 . Revise guidelines and submit copy to director of curriculum and instruction and principal by December 1, 1972.
10 . Be prepared to discuss guidelines with building staff by December 2, 1972.

The above performance objectives and action plans have been mutually agreed to by the undersigned.

_____ Submitted by: _____
      Date   Teacher

_____ Approved by: _____
      Date   Supervisor

MAINTAINING A RECORD OF OBJECTIVES

When the administrator receives the first copy of the teacher's Statement of Performance Objectives and when his suggestions for assisting the teacher have been agreed to, the information is recorded on the statement and is maintained in the administrative notebook as long range goals and short range objectives.

This operations notebook consists of a three-ring binder with dividers for each administrator and director in the district. All objectives should be grouped under their appropriate classification for each administrator, that is, all problem-solving and professional skill objectives for a particular administrator should be grouped together. Supportive materials, such as financial documents and Needs Assessment Reports, are filed in the rear of the notebook under supportive materials.

REPORTING RESULTS

It is appropriate at this time to turn our attention to the report which is used by supervisors in controlling and evaluating results of their staff. This report is the crux of school management by objectives. This report describes what has happened, what is happening, and what the administrator must make happen if the objectives are to be achieved. Each objective, depending upon how it is expressed, provides the administrator with interim opportunities to effect action to achieve objectives and to evaluate results once the objective has been reached.[1] (A sample of a completed Performance Appraisal Review form which is keyed to the Statement of Performance Objectives is shown on the following pages.)

The method for reporting results advocated by the author consists of a simple form. On the left side of the form, a description of the specific act to be achieved with minimum standards of acceptance is indicated. The left side is developed according to those objectives which were achieved above, on and below plan. On the right side of the form, the results achieved or in the process of being achieved are indicated with explanation. A result summary appears in this form. In the box provided with a plus symbol, the number of objectives which were achieved above plan is indicated. In the middle box without any symbol, the number of objectives which were achieved on plan is indicated. In the box provided with a minus symbol, the number of objectives which were achieved below plan should be indicated.

Also indicated in the Performance Appraisal Review form should be activities which the supervisor agrees to perform in order to assist the appraisee in reaching his objectives.

At the lower portion of the last page of the Performance Appraisal Review, the appraisee and the appraiser should sign the document.

SUMMARY

The responsibility for the implementation of school management by objectives and the objective-centered approach to performance

---

[1] Dale D. McAnkey, *"How to Manage by Results"*, American Management Association, New York, N.Y., 1967, p. 81.

appraisal should rest with the superintendent or an assistant superintendent. Operational procedures for setting objectives must be established for the smooth transition of the program. One important aspect of the objective-centered approach to performance appraisal is that once there is mutual agreement by the administrator and teacher, the objectives should be recorded in writing. The Statement of Performance Objectives should be maintained in an operations handbook which is kept by all supervisors. Performance results should be recorded on a Performance Appraisal Review form.

WYANDANCH PUBLIC SCHOOLS

PROFESSIONAL PERFORMANCE REVIEW

<u>MRS. MARY WILKERSON</u>
Name

<u>ELEMENTARY TEACHER</u>
Position

School Year 1971 – 1972

One copy of this form is to be retained by the Individual whose performance is being reviewed. One copy should be retained by his immediate supervisor and one copy should be forwarded to the chief school officer.

Figure 8-1 PERFORMANCE APPRAISAL REVIEW FORM

Name of Appraisor	Next Review Date
Mr. James Butler	January 15, 1973
Position Title	Location
Elementary Principal	Milton L. Olive Elementary School

Performance Objectives	Progress Review
ON PLAN: 3.1 To design a procedure for adjusting to team members' absence in order to reduce the need for substitute teachers. (Minimal level of acceptable standard is determined by the number of substitutes hired during the present school year which should account for no more than 7 per teacher per team)	If the present rate of teachers' absence continues, our team will achieve this objective either on plan or above plan. Presently, only four teachers were absent for the period which necessitated hiring substitute teachers.
Below Plan: 3.2 To implement a lab-centered 4th grade science course so that a minimum of 60% of the 4th grade students will successfully complete the course.	Weekly tests indicate that if the present rate continues only 30% of the 4th grade students will successfully complete the science course. I will need assistance with this objective.

Revised/Modified Objectives and Action Plan:

3.2   Short Range Objective
   1. Develop plans for establishing science lab in building by January 5, 1972.

   2. Design guidelines for use of science lab by teachers and students by January 20, 1972.

   3. Relate classroom science activities to science lab and provide opportunities for all students to use the lab at least 4 hours per week.

   4. After the science lab has been in use for one month, meet with Director of Curriculum and Instruction to discuss the results.

New Objectives:

PROFESSIONAL PERFORMANCE REVIEW

Name of Appraisee Mrs. Mary Wilkerson	Review Date November 15, 1972
Position Title Elementary Teacher	School Milton L. Olive Elementary School

Performance Objectives	Progress Review
ABOVE PLAN: 1.5 I will visit each student's home and confer with his parents. This objective will be successfully achieved if I visit the homes of all of my students.	I have visited the homes of four-teen of my students. Each visit took approximately one hour.
2.1 To teach a minimum of two (2) health lessons a week from November 1, 1972 to June 28, 1973.	By teaming, I was able to teach three and sometimes four health lessons per week with excellent results as indicated on weekly tests.
ON PLAN: 1.4 I will use the problem-solving conference as a technique for solving problems. A minimum of 75% of the students must give a satisfactory rating to this technique as determined by a survey.	This technique has been fully instituted as a means for solving individual and group problems in my class. An informal survey indicates that the students are very elated about this new tech-que.
4.1 To attend a minimum of 90% of in-service workshops on the psychodynamics of teaching.	At the rate I am going I should be able to attend more than 90% of the workshops - I have attended all five of the workshops presented thus far.
4.2 To attend the fourth conference of the National Association for the Individualization of Instruction on Nov. 7-9, 1972.	I attended the fourth conference of NAII and enjoyed it immensely.
To prepare guidelines in individualizing and humanizing instruction which will be reviewed by the members of my team for use by Dec. 1, 1972.	I am presently drafting the outline for the guidelines.

PROFESSIONAL PERFORMANCE REVIEW

Name of Appraisee: Mrs. Mary Wilkerson	Review Date November 15, 1972
Position Title Elementary Teacher	School Milton L. Olive Elementary School
Performance Objectives	Progress Review

Above Plan:

1.3 I will improve my questioning techniques with my class by:

    a. Asking the questions first, then calling on the students to answer.

    b. Use the student's response to question as a springboard for dialogue among the rest of the class.

    c. Use a maximum of two sentences to elicit response from the students.

    d. Keep my dialogue to a maximum of twenty five percent.

The success of this objective is determined by a satisfactory rating from the principal.

On two occasions the principal came into my class unannounced and observed my teaching performance for proper questioning techniques. He rated each performance "excellent."

On Plan:

1.3 I will develop a series of reading tapes and worksheets to reinforce skills in decoding already taught. The success of this objective will be determined by a 75% increase in students' performance in decoding skills after the materials have been in use for a period of four months.

All tapes and worksheets for the reading series have been completed. All suggestions recommended by the principal and curriculum associate have been made. Clerk-typist has completed typing the printed materials. The tapes and worksheets have been implemented in the reading program for one week.

1.1 I will visit the classrooms of several exemplary teachers so that I can observe their teaching styles and learn how they maintain classroom conduct. The success of this objective will be determined by a satisfactory rating from the principal.

Although I have not observed as many exemplary teachers as I projected, those which I did observe were indeed impressive. I have learned much from these teachers. The principal has indicated that I am doing "very well."

SUMMARY OF APPRAISAL RESULTS

Following is the overall appraisal of the appraisee's total effectiveness on the job in in terms of number of objectives achieved or are in the process of being achieved:

+3	6	-1

The immediate supervisor agrees to perform the following activities to assist the appraisee in achieving his objectives:

1. Assist in developing ESEA Title I proposal for establishing science lab by January 5, 1973.

2. Follow up on science order in Central Administration office.

3. Request the chief school officer to grant one (1) visitation day to visit the Holloway Elementary School in Mayflower, L.I. to observe their science lab.

4. To request the director of curriculum and instruction to meet with the appraisee at least two hours a week for a period of three weeks to discuss problem-solving techniques in science.

No more assistance is warranted at this time.

The above performance objectives and action plans which may be new, revised or modified have been mutually agreed to by the undersigned:

Date	Submitted by:
November 12, 1972	Mary
Date	Approved by:
November 12, 1972	

NINE

Improving Performance: Appraisal Counseling

In education, performance appraisal is frequently looked upon as an evaluation which affects only the teacher being appraised; it's an important influence upon the administrator and cannot be over-emphasized. One of its greatest benefits is to encourage each administrator to do more analytical and constructive thinking about the performance of his teachers. It should force him to face up to some of his own prejudices and biases. It should also help him to question whether his feelings may be without foundation, unreasonable and/or unfair. The performance appraisal process should help the administrator to be more specific about his staff's strong and weak points, and be able to perceive that each teacher is different and should be treated bearing these differences in mind. Administrators must understand that they inject a bit of themselves into every appraisal. Administrators must also understand that the appraisal process involves not only evaluation of the teacher but also of the administrator. His effectiveness is predicated on how successful his teachers are, with his assistance, in reaching their objectives. This chapter has been designed to give a rationale for appraising performance, to define the post-appraisal conference, to state the purposes of the post-appraisal conference, to elaborate on two types of conferences, to cite problem areas when appraising and counseling, to identify some "do's and don't's" when conducting a conference, to focus on how to ask effective questions, to denote preliminary steps before the conference, to mention how to conduct the appraisal conference, and to comment on how to conclude and follow through on a conference.

RATIONALE FOR APPRAISING THE PERFORMANCE
OF SCHOOL PERSONNEL

1. The administrator can improve the achievement of his team, department, and school building or system by periodically appraising the performance of his staff; and by appraising, directing, guiding, counseling and assisting at various appropriate times.

2. The administrator should manage and maintain the performance appraising program as systematically as any other program. He must plan, organize, guide and control the activities of the program. He is obligated to motivate teachers to plan, organize, start and continue the activities of the program. Performance appraising should be a more humane and effective way to performance evaluation and development.

3. The teacher should know: (a) what is expected of him; (b) how he is doing; and, (c) that he will be provided with assistance if he needs it.

4. The logical and most appropriate approach to the performance appraisal program is to assess performance in relation to results expected as previously agreed upon by the administrator and the teacher. By so doing, the *what* and the *how much* was achieved by the teacher is crystal clear.

5. For the purpose of improving the personal development of teachers, it is necessary to determine why the performance of the teacher was unsatisfactory. From this information the development and training program in an area of need can be ascertained.

6. There is much of value in the performance appraisal program since it is a system based on a mutual or joint process during which the teacher evaluates himself and the administrator evaluates the teacher. Improved performance results when the teacher sees for himself where the fault lies and then does something about it.

7. The administrator should be familiar with the teacher's achievements; however, it is possible that the teacher can also enlighten the administrator on some points.

8. A great deal of the teacher's performance development can be accomplished on the job.

9. All professional development is self-development. However, as the teacher has the responsibility of achieving needed self-development,

it is the responsibility of the administrator and the school system to provide appropriate counseling, opportunities, resources, and time for the teacher's personal development.

10. The performance appraisal should not only include assessment of the performance of the teacher, but should also include a review of the services provided by the administrator to assist the teacher in achieving his objectives. Just as the teacher is self-appraising his own performance, so should the administrator assess his own performance with respect to his contributions to the teacher's results.

WHAT IS THE POST-APPRAISAL CONFERENCE?

The post-appraisal conference is a meeting between two or more individuals for the purpose of presenting and explaining essential information about the job requirements, discussing and pooling ideas and arriving at recommendations for solving problems, setting objectives, developing action plans, and improving performance. It embodies investigations, discussions and communications between the administrator and the teacher on matters which are of mutual interest and concern before decisions are made either by the teacher or the administrator. The procedure for the conference is characterized by an objective unbiased discussion free of extraneous items, conducted in a climate free of emotional conflict. The technique of the conference is designed to encourage participatory decision-making, effective thinking and frank expression by the parties involved in the conference. When administrators use the post-appraisal conference as a means for appraising and counseling, it produces improved and more acceptable decisions, it decreases the number and severity of school related problems and it satisfies the personal needs of the teachers participating in important matters affecting them.

PURPOSES OF POST-APPRAISAL CONFERENCE

Post appraisal conferences are initiated for the following reasons:

1. Guiding and Directing the Teacher in Setting Objectives

The very first task in goal setting is for the administrator to arrange a time and place to guide the teacher in the setting of his objectives. The teacher should be well aware of the administrator's major goals;

he should arrive for his appointment with appropriate notes. At this time, the administrator should explain to the teacher the general conditions under which he will be working and broadly indicate the professional responsibilities of the teacher in terms of the overall expectations of the school district. By so doing, the administrator is placing the teacher "on track." It is also desirable for the administrator to suggest some of the areas where objective setting might be desirable for the oncoming school year. The teacher is then asked to consider the information presented to him, carefully review his job description and report back at a stated time to suggest some performance objectives for him to set out to achieve. This takes us to the next purpose or reason for the post appraisal conference.

2. Negotiating on Objectives or Mutually Agreeing on Objectives

Before the administrator and teacher meet to negotiate or mutually agree on objectives, the teacher should be given time to think through his area of responsibility. The teacher should analyze his whole operation so that he can arrive at objectives which he is reasonably certain he will achieve. Before setting his objectives, it is desirable for him to consider the three broad areas of objective setting and to develop a plan for meeting each area.

The negotiating on objectives or mutually agreeing on objectives takes place at the individual conference when the administrator reviews the proposed Statement of Performance Objectives recommended by the teacher. Essentially this conference is a coaching seminar designed primarily for counseling the teacher in setting objectives and for sharpening up his proposed Statement of Performance Objectives. The teacher should be given adequate time and opportunity to explain and discuss his proposal to the administrator. The administrator should at all cost avoid suggesting ready-made objectives to the teacher. If the participatory decision making process is to be maintained, then teachers must develop their own objectives. The role of the teacher should be relatively active and the role of the administrator should be relatively passive within the framework of his own responsibilities depending upon the extent to which the teacher has achieved his objectives. During the conference the following questions should be considered:

1. Were the performance objectives stated in specific and observable terms?

2. Did the objectives contain the conditions, the acts and the minimal standards?
3. Were practical and realistic standards identified for each objective?
4. Were any objectives omitted which are important for the successful performance of the position?
5. Do the objectives meet all of the requirements outlined in Chapter Four.

One common fault which this author has observed when school management by objectives is being implemented is that some teachers have a tendency to set "low risk" bearing goals. The administrator should be on the alert during this conference session for these "low risk" bearing goals. He should take this opportunity to negotiate more challenging goals. At times, however, a teacher may have set his objectives too high ("high risk" setting goals). When this occurs, the administrator should counsel the teacher to develop an objective more in line with reality. An effective way to do this is by saying to the teacher, "I appreciate your eagerness to do an outstanding job; however, I believe that at this time it would be best for you to perform the following (lower) objective. I will be satisfied and I believe you will be too." If the teacher insists he can achieve the higher objectives, then by all means he should be permitted to do so.

Let us assume that the teacher insisted on setting the high risk bearing objectives, and, as a result of his attempt to achieve this objective, a problem occurred. This leads us to the next reason for conducting the post-appraisal conference.

3. Problem-Solving Need Because of Failure to Achieve Professional Skill Objectives

When a problem occurs, it is usually best fot the administrator to convene a meeting with an individual teacher or a group (such as a department or team) in order to reach a decision for solving the problem. Unlike the nondirective conference, the administrator takes an active role in this conference and he alone must make the final decision for solving the problem.

There are five phases to the problem-solving conference:

1. Presentation of the problem.

Omitting any reference to responsibilities for creating the problem, the administrator attempts to define the problem by presenting illustrative pertinent information. After the problem has been specifically defined, the administrator explains the ground rules and sets the limitations for arriving at solutions for the problem. In the presentation of the problem by the administrator, it is imperative that the individual teacher or group of teachers who have been called in to assist in arriving at a solution to the problem have a clear and uniform understanding of the problem and of their roles in reaching a solution.

2. Discussion of the problem.

The administrator initiates the discussion of the problem, stimulates discussion when it lags, controls it if it gets out of hand and organizes it to reach a final consensus of opinion. He starts the discussion by asking leading questions which can be easily answered. Then he directs specific questions to particular teachers from whom he can expect ready answers. The administrators should listen carefully and probe for ideas and further thoughts on the questions. He calls on teachers who have something special to offer in addition to supplying facts and ideas not presented by the group. The administrator must talk little, listen much, and think a lot. He controls the conference by keeping the discussions relevant to the problem. While the discussion is taking place, he makes a visual presentation (usually on a blackboard) of the ideas and suggestions as they emanate from the teachers.

3. Evaluation of ideas.

The administrator assists the teacher in evaluating the results of the discussion by weighing, classifying and synthesizing the ideas and suggestions recommended.

4. Summary of the conference.

When the substance of the discussion is over, the administrator makes a summation, emphasizing the points on which there is a consensus of opinion but also recognizing other ideas where there was not a consensus.

5. Arriving at a solution to the problem.

The administrator carefully and methodically examines and accepts all of the ideas and suggestions offered to him and renders his opinion of the best alternative to solving the problem.

Let us assume that the problem is resolved, and after ten weeks go by, it is time for a periodic review of performance.

6. Periodic review of performance.

At this time the teacher's performance is evaluated against the objectives which he set for himself. During this non-directed conference the administrator's attitude should be that of an undestanding coach or counselor and the entire conference should be relaxed.

IDENTIFYING TWO TYPES OF CONFERENCES

In objective-centered approach to appraisal, every educator has some degree of responsibility for responding to his colleagues. To fulfill this responsibility it is necessary to identify the various types of conferences used within the school complex, thus maintaining the two-way communication network so vital to successful operation of the schools.

DIRECTED CONFERENCE

The directed conference is planned and led by the administrator to solve problems which have occurred in the process of achieving objectives. He knows precisely why he has convened the conference and he usually wants answers to specific questions. Whenever this type of conference is planned, it is usually possible to anticipate the time required. It is also possible to brief the participants so that the necessary data is available.

In the objective-centered appraisal approach, the directed conference is needed when teachers have not performed according to what has been mutually agreed to and an explanation is needed by the administrator in order to put the teacher "on track." When the traditional appraisal program was implemented, this conference usually dominated; however, when school management by objectives is in operation, the non-directed conference usually dominates because of the desirability for equal participation.

The administrator gives a short illustrated lecture on the problem in which he analyzes and explains to the teacher the problems which he would like to get him to consider. The administrator attempts to orient the teacher psychologically to present his ideas, suggestions and recommendations.

The administrator also discusses the method he would like the teacher to use in arriving at alternatives for solving the problem.

This method for solving problems [1] should involve the citation of the problems by the administrator, after which he initiates the conference by leading with a question such as, "All right, you have heard the problem, who has an alternative or idea for resolving the problem?" This sort of question permits everyone who has something to offer to speak out. Not all of the teachers will be willing to talk during the conference; in this case the administrator must be patient, stimulate discussion by offering new ideas and suggestions. At times the administrator will have to call on individual teachers to get their ideas.

The administrator must develop the knack for listening, talking only when necessary and probing for ideas if he is truly going to become an effectual leader of educators.

Evaluation is an essential part of directed conferences. It is at this time that priorities are weighed and classified. It is from this past that the administrator begins to arrive at a decision to solve the problem.

THE NON-DIRECTED CONFERENCE

The non-directed conference has been mutually planned and agreed to by the administrator and teacher. This conference is more ambitious and is usually conducted for a longer time period than the directed conference. The primary reason for this conference is to achieve understanding and to build confidence. Frequently the conference is held to assist a teacher in overcoming difficulty with a particular objective and for conducting the periodic review of peformance. During this conference the administrator tries not to lead the discussion but encourages the teacher to talk freely and frankly about matters which are of concern to him by asking pertinent questions as suggested further on in this chapter. If the teacher is not free to express his feelings,

---

[1] The author advocates the directed conference for solving problems. However, the non-directed conference has also been used effectively in arriving at solutions to certain school problems, particularly those of a human relations nature.

attitudes and ideas, then the non-directed conference will lapse into the directed conference and the reason for calling the conference in the first place will have failed.

The non-directed conference calls for a considerable amount of skill flexibility, self-control and understanding on the part of the administrator. The non-directed conference is not a session for random discussion, nor need it be entirely unplanned either by the teacher or administrator. In fact, it is highly recommended that notes be brought to the conference in order to discuss some specific details. It must be emphasized here that conference domination or unilateral control by the administrator is inappropriate whenever the reason for the conference is to achieve a mutual understanding. The teacher must be free to say whatever he wants to say without fear of reprisal or reprimand. The administrator should be a responsive listener if he is to provide the teacher with boosts to self-confidence and self-awareness. In school management by objectives, the nondirected conference embodies the human side of operating the schools.

The directed and non-directed conference each have some distinct features. In practice it is common for both types of conferences to merge. The effective administrator will make the most out of this opportunity afforded him and change from one type of conference to another according to the time and need.

PROBLEM AREAS WHEN APPRAISING AND COUNSELING

The primary problem area when appraising and counseling is that it is a human activity. A school is complex and by its very nature already beset with a variety of built-in human problems that occur when the administrator attempts to evaluate, judge, develop, modify and change the behavior of a teacher. The degree to which the administrator's judgment is purely objective will determine the extent to which human judgment and personality problems can be decreased or even eliminated.

For years, it has been known that the personality and expectations of the administrator create problems during the post-appraisal conference. There are also problems which may occur as a result of the school environment which must be resolved one way or another: unclear objectives, lack of action plans for reaching objectives, lack of job classification, poor training in school management by objectives, lack of motivational techniques on the part of the administrator, the reputations of both administrator and teacher. The following constitute some potential problem areas in the post-appraisal conference:

- Overcoming the natural biases of both administrators and teachers.
- Evoking of characteristics and traits for the particular professional position.
- Reaching an agreement on a definition of each characteristic and trait when objectives are set.
- Deciding which characteristics and traits are to be appraised (very touchy affair).
- Concentrating on performance in relation to results rather than dealing with judgments of educators.

However, most of the above pitfalls and problems can be avoided if the following antidotes are employed successfully:

- Administrator and teacher mutually agree on objectives and record them in writing.
- Administrator and teacher jointly agree to how performance will be evaluated.
- Administrator avoids criticizing and employs counseling and coaching techniques to get improved performance.
- Teacher has supportive data for his self-appraisal report.
- Appraisal of the teacher's performance is based on results achieved rather than on his personality.
- Teacher develops his own objectives to support and reach the long range goals established by the administrator.

Both administrators and teachers should be familiar with the common pitfalls and problems associated with appraising and counseling. The chief school officer cannot effectively implement an objective-centered approach to performance appraisal unless both administrators and teachers make every attempt to circumvent the pitfalls and problems that are inherent in the program.

"DO'S AND DON'T'S" WHEN CONDUCTING A CONFERENCE

Do's:

1. Keep the individual or group on the subject, moving them forward in an orderly way through the discussion to arrive at specific ideas and solutions to problems.

2. If the conference lags, offer new ideas in order to give the teacher a fresh look at the discussion or problem under consideration.
3. Be patient. If the discussion or questions are thought-provoking, the teacher will need sufficient time to think.
4. Be a good listener. This is done effectively by interjecting in the conversation, "Why?" "Tell me more about your objectives." "What do you hope to accomplish?"
5. Jot down comments and important points.
6. Summarize before the conference terminates; it is always appropriate to recap mutual agreements.

Don't's:

1. Dictate overtly or implicitly by telling an individual or group what they should do or think.
2. Manipulate the teacher by subtly trying to get predetermined conclusions.
3. Talk too much, if the purpose of the conference is to get participation in the management of the affairs of the school. The administrator should talk less and listen more.
4. Display bias for your own ideas and suggestions by subtly getting the teacher to react favorably to your recommendations.
5. Resort to phrases such as "you haven't . . .", "I suppose you would agree . . . ", "I disagree with you . . .".

BRIDGING THE COMMUNICATION GAP DURING THE POST-APPRAISAL CONFERENCE

There is a serious communication gap existing between the teachers and administrators. One reason for this is that traditionally downward communication has been employed by autocratic administrators and few if any effective avenues have been provided for communication in the upward and sideward directions. In fact, so serious is this communication gap that it has perpetuated and enlarged the division between teachers and administrators. Most administrators are or should be aware that the reason for mandated collective bargaining in some states is due to this communication gap. However, by the very nature of the objective-centered approach to appraisal which fosters the participatory decision-making process, an attempt is made to eliminate this gap entirely by its multi-directional communication focus. Even through this process, administrators must make a conscious effort to employ effective communication techniques, or there will still exist a serious flaw in the professional performance appraisal program. One way in which administrators can enhance their ability to coach and counsel is by learning the skill of asking pertinent questions.

ESTABLISH A CLIMATE OF CONFIDENCE

Administrators who continue to practice the authoritative controlled relationship with their staff are primarily responsible for the fear and distrust which exists between administrators and teachers. Ernest D. Nathan who is vice president of Florenz, Inc., in Detroit, Michigan, states that:

> . . . where distrust or fear exists on either side of the conversa-
> tion, the likelihood of understanding is remote. Obviously, a
> climate of confidence cannot be created instantaneously. It must
> develop over time from continued contact.[2]

Mr. Nathan further adds:

> How a question is asked is often more important than what is
> asked . . . you can ask them in a way that immediately chal-
> lenges the respondent and raises his boiling point, or you can
> ask them with a tone that will encourage confidence and resulting
> understanding.[3]

The tone of the administrator's voice when conferring with a teacher during the post-appraisal conference is probably the most important indicator of how the question will be received. If the administrator shouts and criticizes during the conference, the teacher will be on the defensive immediately. He will most likely attempt to defend himself the best way he can, by using the same weapon of criticism, by displaying the anger on his face and raising his own voice; or, if he is really on the defensive, he might even strike at the administrator which occurred once at a negotiation session in a school district on Long Island, N.Y. On the other hand, an administrator's "smile of

---

[2] Eugene Raudsepp, "Bridge the Gap with Questions," *Machine Design*, Penton Publication, Cleveland, Ohio, 1970, pp. 32-35.

[3] *Ibid.*

appreciation" can help to ensure good receptivity for questions during the conference.

The physical conduct of the administrator during the conference will in one way of another determine the teacher's attitude toward responding to questions. For example, if the administrator looks indifferent or seems to have other things on his mind during the conference, he certainly will not induce a teacher to have much enthusiasm in answering questions.

Mr. Nathan recommends the two following points to enhance mutual understanding and communication:

1. The *administrator* should not be satisfied with the response to the primary question regardless of what is stated. He should always try to come back with a secondary question, such as: "Why is that?" or "How do you happen to feel that way about it?"

2. The *administrator* should not slam the door of communication by agreeing or disagreeing flatly with the *teacher's* response. The door should be kept open with noncommital reinforcement like: "Uh-hum. I see. Oh, yes. I see what you mean." The *administrator* can also simply repeat the *teacher's* response exactly as it was given. Still another method to keep the communication doors open is simply by saying nothing—and remaining silent until the *teacher* says what is on his mind. Silence by an *administrator* during the post-appraisal conference is often the signal for the *teacher* to speak.[4]

HOW TO ASK QUESTIONS DURING THE POST-APPRAISAL CONFERENCE

The way an administrator poses a question to a teacher will determine the extent to which the questions will be received. Questions may fall into two categories:[5] (1) functional questions, which are interrogative statements designed to get "acceptable" answers that are solutions to problems; (2) non-functional questions, which are interrogative statements which do not get "acceptable" solutions to problems. They

---

[4] *Ibid.* The author has substituted the word *administrator* for *manager* and *teacher* for *subordinate* in the original text of Ernest D. Nathan.

[5] *Ibid.*

in essence do not work. Ernest D. Nathan describes these two categories of questions as follows:

FUNCTIONAL QUESTIONS

Direct questions use who, what, when, where and how to invite the teacher to express himself openly. Examples: "How do you think we can use the remedial reading teacher?" "What do you think of Dr. Anderson's book on nongraded education?" "Do you have any ideas as to how we can provide for individual differences?" These questions are usually to the point and invite the teacher's cooperation. What is implied in these questions is respect for his professional abilities and judgement applied to solving problems.

Leading questions give non-restrictive direction to the response. Examples: "How did you get your teacher aide to correct the IPI score sheets promptly?" "How did you go about teaching IPI to new teachers?"

Planted answer questions invite the teacher to give his own opinion although there is an implied direction along lines which the administrator feels will lead to effective solutions of the problems. This question also implies that the administrator is willing to accept criticisms and other ideas. Examples: "How about using Dr. Pino's approach to differentiated staffing?" "What are your ideas on the implementation of the British Infant School in our first three grades?"

Unemotional questions appeal to reason and evoke very little or no feelings. Examples: "What would be the first phase for implementing school management by objectives in this school district?" "Do you have any thoughts about the high absentee rate of students?"

Invitation-to-participate questions let the teacher know that he can make a real contribution by expressing his own views. Examples: "I need your help on this." "Whom do you recommend for team leader for Beta Team?" "Can we improve on our nongraded program?"

Off-the-hook questions allow the teacher to decline a request without losing face. Examples: "I can't afford to attend the Fourth Conference of The National Association For The Individualization Of Instruction. Could you do so for me?" "I don't suppose your team will be able to come to school an hour early for planning purposes?"

Invitation-to-comply questions involve a request with the sting taken out of it by using the terms "okay" or "right". Example: "I know this objective is difficult to formulate but it will give both of us directions. O.K.?"

Invitation-to-feedback questions enable the administrator to check on the teacher's understanding of an assignment or objective. Example: "Is it understood that you will set an objective to measure effective teaching skills in the area of science and that you will present me with a draft of your objective by the end of this week?"

Opening-the-feelings question invites the teacher to reveal his true feelings about a matter. Examples: "I understand that you didn't go along with your team decision—what specifically did you disagree with?" "Do you think I was unfair with you?"

Bring-out-bashful ideas questions ask for elaboration. Examples: "I am not certain that I understand you. Give me an example." "What objective do you think we should work together to attain this school year?"

NON-FUNCTIONAL QUESTIONS

Squelcher questions force the teacher to adopt a point of view with which he doesn't agree, or which force him to conform to a preconceived pattern. Examples: "None of your ideas have worked—what makes you think that you can solve this problem?" "Your team has not been successful in implementing team teaching in the past—why do you think they will in the future?" Such questions usually reduce the teacher's feeling of confidence and may stifle any initiative.

Dead-end questions drive the teacher into a corner no matter what his answer may be. Example: "What makes you think that course of action taken by you and the other members of your team was the right one?"

Emotionally-heated questions evoke negative feelings in the teacher. Examples: "We have had several studies completed in this area, why do you insist on another study?" "I've listened to you long enough—can you get down to specifics, so that I will know what you are trying to get at?"

Trick questions appear to ask for a frank opinion but actually leave little choice for a teacher to come up with a solution. Example: "What should we do about the new teacher in your department? Should we fire her or transfer her to another school in the district?"

Minor questions simply invite compliance. Example: "This is the way to do this. Do you agree?"

Kill-the-idea questions limit any consideration for developing the idea further. Example: "That is an excellent idea, but that won't work in this school. I think we should try this approach instead. Don't you agree?"[6]

THE PRELIMINARY STEPS
BEFORE THE CONFERENCE

Procedures and skill for conducting either a directed or non-directed conference will vary with the administrator according to the time available before, during, and after the conference. The following are preliminary steps which should take place before conducting any conference.

REVIEW ALL ESSENTIALS

Before the conference and particularly during the periodic assessment of performance, the administrator should have consulted his notes from the previous conference. He should also review all notes made during the teacher's classroom observation. If a directed conference is to be initiated, the administrator should review all of the available information at his disposal in order to ask the appropriate questions. During this phase of the preparation for the conference, the administrator who is conducting the conference should do his homework thoroughly.

PLANNING FOR THE CONFERENCE

The nature and amount of planning depends largely on three factors. They are:

1. Whether the conference is to be directed or non-directed.

2. Whether the administrator initiates it or is informed of it in sufficient time to permit planning.

3. Having done sufficient advance thinking about the problem, the administrator can spend his time during the conference listening, probing and observing.

---

[6] *Ibid.*

NOTIFY THE TEACHER ABOUT THE CONFERENCE

It is always appropriate to give the teacher a reminder notice about the conference, even though the administrator may be certain that the teacher is aware of the conference. When formulating the notice, the time, place, approximate duration and reason for the conference should be spelled out. Some administrators have been known to use conference notification as a psychological weapon by omitting the reason for the conference. The teacher who gets a notice without a declaration of the reason tends to take a negative point of view and often wonders, "What have I done now?" In school management by objectives this sort of psychological warfare has no place.

THE SETTING FOR THE CONFERENCE

A successful conference depends in part on a suitable setting. Some items which should be considered are:

1. Privacy and Comfortable Environment

Whenever possible the conference should be held in a private office with comfortable chairs and table. The author brings to mind one principal who ordered a couch and a coffee table for his office to conduct meetings not only with teachers, but with irate parents. Sometimes coffee is served by the administrator to relax the teacher. Some administrators may prefer to conduct the conference in the privacy of a place away from the school setting. This is particularly true when the conference is of a directed nature.

2. An Atmosphere of Leisure

There should be sufficient time to conduct the nondirected conference. For this reason it is advisable to hold these conferences when there are two free periods back-to-back. The directed conference can usually be completed within 15 or 20 minutes. However, the administrator should always convey the impression that he has plenty of time.

3. Interruptions

Interruptions can seriously affect the conference by destroying the continuity which has developed as a result of the interaction between the administrator and teacher. In view of this it is desirable to provide for holding telephone calls and messages for the duration of the conference. It may be advisable for a sign to be posted indicating "In Conference—Do Not Disturb" on the office where the conference is being conducted.

PREPARING FOR THE POST-APPRAISAL CONFERENCE

The administrator is likely to conduct a successful post-appraisal conference when he is well prepared attitudinally as well as intellectually.

1. Be objective in appraising the performance of the teacher. Evaluate results achieved against results expected in specific "observable" terms. At this time, existing circumstances or emergencies should be considered which prevented anticipated results.

2. When analyzing the teacher's performance, base it on observations which are derived from watching, listening and inquiry for the purpose of getting complete and accurate information.

3. Keep alert for important factors in the work situation which give insight into the teacher's on-the-job performance.

4. Develop an effective way for recording the teacher's observation, so that this can be used as a gauge for analyzing and evaluating.

5. Use a form similar to the one shown in Figure 9-1 as a guide for progressing through the conference.

6. The administrator should evaluate not only the performance of the teacher, but also his own, in terms of how the teacher is being assisted in meeting his objectives.

CONDUCTING THE POST-APPRAISAL CONFERENCE

The most humane aspect of school management by objectives is evident in the post-appraisal conference. The following guidelines are offered for conducting the post-appraisal conference:

1. After the administrator "breaks the ice," the first subject to

Check each item as completed

ACTION TO BE COMPLETED	KEY POINTS
Teacher/Administrator	
1. Ask the teacher to think about the long range goals disseminated to the staff. He should then be prepared to discuss those goals in line with his own area of responsibility. *Schedule a time for guiding and directing the teacher for setting objectives.* _____ Date and Time	Explain to the teacher that this is the first step in the objective-centered approach to performance appraisal and it is designed to improve his performance and provide him with an opportunity to participate in decisions which will affect him.
2. Hold the conference.	The administrator should first discuss the general condition under which the teacher will be working and in a broad way, indicate his overall expectation in terms of long range objectives. Also indicate to the teacher where the administrator thinks objectives might be set for the ensuing school year. At this meeting the administrator can also cover other things on his mind; matters such as relationships in school, opportunities, school-related personnel problems, etc. Budget approximately one hour for this conference.
3. Ask teacher to jot down information discussed in the conference, carefully review his own area of responsibility and decide on some priorities. The teacher should then be instructed to prepare his proposed objectives and submit them to the administrator prior to the scheduled conference for review before the conference takes place. *Schedule the conference for reviewing the proposed objectives.*	Normally, these objectives will fall in four types: Professional Skill objectives, problem-solving objectives, innovative objectives and personal development objectives. Direct as well as indirect objectives should be set. Each objective must contain an action plan which will spell out the procedural steps for reaching the objectives. Usually six to eight objectives are set.
4. Hold the conference to review the proposed objectives.	The administrator should review the teacher's objectives in detail, then offer his own suggestions or changes. Once a mutual agreement has been reached over the objectives and action plans, and all modifications are reached, the administrator should inquire as to what he can do to assist the teacher in achieving the objectives. These comments should be recorded in writing. Budget at least forty-five minutes for a conference that will be free of interruptions.

Figure 9-1

ACTION TO BE COMPLETED	KEY POINTS
5. Using the statement of objectives and action plans, the teacher sets out to achieve his objectives. *Schedule the post appraisal conference.* _____ Date and Time	The administrator should cross check the teacher s performance with the statement of objectives and action plans to identify: 1. areas for development which need attention — 2. areas of strengths and job accomplishments. At this time, the administrator should regard this "check" only tentative until after the post appraisal has taken place and the administrator has had an opportunity to explore the teacher's self-appraisal because he might desire to alter his own appraisal. Then checks should take place frequently throughout each appraisal period. Notes and comments should be regarded so that they are not forgotten. Reinforce good results with compliments as they occur. Use poor results as a platform for coaching and counseling.
6. Hold the post appraisal conference beginning with the self-appraisal report. Coach and counsel the teacher.	Questions which should be considered are: Is the teacher meeting his objectives? Should his objective and/or action-plan be amended or revised? Should the objective be deleted? is the administrator providing proper assistance to enable the teacher to reach the objectives? The administrative objectives should be: 1. to reach a common understanding of the teachers performance. 2. to provide appropriate recognition for above, on and below plan performance; 3. to arrive at a mutual agreement on areas for improvment.

Notes:

be discussed during the conference should be a comparison of the results expected with results achieved. By reviewing the teacher's Performance Appraisal Review form, this can be fairly easily accomplished. Although the directed conference is led by the administrator, his role is to have the teacher pinpoint areas of low achievement. He also guides the conference so that definite conclusions are reached, and in the end the teacher is well aware of his standing with the administrator.

2. The administrator should encourage the teacher to do most of the talking at the conference. It is the teacher's development with which the administrator should be concerned; therefore, the administrator should provide the impetus that motivates the teacher to speak freely. The administrator must remember that his primary role is to coach, to guide and to assist the teacher in achieving his objectives.

3. The discussion of the objectives should develop from pertinent information so that the administrator and teacher mutually agree on specific objectives to be achieved by the next appraisal conference. It may be necessary to convene other meetings in order to provide more time to gather essential data to arrive at appropriate objectives.

4. Documentation is not a dominant feature of the appraisal conference; however, notes must be taken so that there is a mutual understanding of the matters discussed.

5. One copy of the Performance Appraisal Review form should be given to the teacher, a copy should be placed in the teacher's placement file and a final copy should be retained by the administrator.

During the post-appraisal conference each objective, standard, and action plan which was mutually agreed to is reviewed. To omit reviewing an objective cannot be condoned and is without justification. During this and subsequent reviews of performance the teacher will be responsible for assessing *all* of the objectives which he set for himself.

During this conference, the following should take place:

a . The teacher evaluates his progress on the objective which he established for himself.
b . The validity of the original objective is evaluated by the administrator and teacher.
c . Necessary modification of the Statement of Performance Objectives is made to make them more practical and realistic.
d . New objectives and action plans are added for the next periodic assessment conference.

This conference should terminate with the administrator and teacher mutually agreeing to the overall assessment of the performance during the period in question. This evaluation, like subsequent periodic evaluations, should be based entirely on results achieved in relation to results expected; personality should not be a factor. Exceptions to this rule are only permitted when personal traits are interfering with the teacher's performance of his objectives.

CONCLUDING THE CONFERENCE

The end of a conference is very important if only because of impressions which may modify the teacher's attitude.

In the directed conference the administrator should summarize the main points covered during the discussion and emphasize those items on which there was agreement. If the conference was called by the teacher in order to help him to arrive at a decision, the administrator merely gives the "pro's" and "con's" for his decision.

It is usually professional courtesy to thank the teacher for his time.

In the nondirected conference, the administrator and teacher should mutually agree to close the conference at a mutually agreeable time. During a conference experienced by the author, the principal who just completed discussing the proposed objectives of a teacher, finished with the following kind words, "Mary, I thought that was not only an extremely meaningful conference but I learned something also. What is your feeling of the conference now?" Mary stated, "I gave and I learned a lot, probably more than I learned in most of my education courses. Are all conferences as good as this one?" The principal retorted, "No! Only mine," and smiled.

ENDING AND DIRECTING THE CONFERENCE

It is highly recommended that a form be devised similar to the one shown under Figure 9-1 for the purpose of keeping the administrator in "touch" as he guides and directs the teachers for setting objectives and reviewing performance. The form should be divided into two parts. The first half of the form should be designated "Action To Be Completed" and the second half of the form should be designated "Key Points." It would also be helpful to indicate sequential steps to be taken by the administrator during the conference.

FOLLOWING THROUGH AFTER THE CONFERENCE

No conference is complete unless an effort is made to follow up on the activities and recommendations made during the conference.

1. Review and rewrite all notes, incorporating important suggestions, recommendations, ideas and resolutions in order to have a detailed outline for the next conference.

2. Make arrangements and record the exact date, time and place to hold the next conference. If an observation or action is necessary to be taken by the administrator, notes should be recorded to this effect.

If the administrator must render a decision concerning a problem discussed in the conference, he should review his notes and synthesize his own ideas or suggestions with those posed by the administrator or teacher, but this should be accomplished after the conference.

REVIEWING AND EVALUATING THE CONFERENCE

When the conference has terminated, the wise administrator should carefully review his notes and mentally check through the conference to assess his effectiveness as a coach or counselor and/or problem solver. In this process he should review what went "wrong" and what went "right," reflecting on what he can do in the next conference to improve his effectiveness as an administrator. Some administrators enjoy writing a self-evaluation report and periodically referring to this report to gauge the progress made in becoming more efficient conferees.

FOLLOWING-UP AFTER THE PERFORMANCE APPRAISAL

Time has a tendency to slip by unnoticed, erasing the results of the best of conferences; therefore, maintaining a program for following-up after post-appraisal conference is not only important to an effective system of school management by objectives, it is essential. The following are some "actions" areas for the effective administrator to bear in mind:

1. Observe the teacher's performance and progress in the fulfillment of his objectives as they occur. Because objective-centered approach erases much of the fear in evaluating education, most teachers will accept and gladly welcome the administrator's visits to their classes.

2. The administrator should comment instantly on good performance and progress as soon as it is noticed. This is an extremely powerful way of motivating and developing a teacher.

3. Correct failure, when possible, in the form of demonstration and discussion. Discussions should take place immediately, thoroughly and constructively so that the teacher will learn how to handle the problem mentioned.

Correction by demonstration and discussion is not as effective as directing improvement because it can lead to fear and discouragement. However, it does have its time and place in many educational situations.

4. Teachers should be encouraged to perform satisfactorily. Old habits have a way of recurring. In order to effect desirable change, the administrator must constantly provide words of encouragement. However, the following must be considered:

a . Administrators should recognize that an encouragement becomes ineffective if no progress is made.
b . Administrators should always attempt to stimulate progress in order to prevent discouragement on the part of the teacher.
c . Administrators should commend the teacher's performance even though it may not be up to his best performance. Any type of improved performance should be recognized by the administrator. The administrator should discuss the performance with the teacher in order to assist in improving the current performances.
d . Administrators should remember to compliment competent performance and progress with objectives; a teacher is likely to strive to achieve more difficult objectives when he is reasonably sure that his efforts are recognized.

5. The administrator should make it a policy to follow up counseling by periodically reviewing the total picture with the teacher, modifying broader goals if they become necessary.

6. The administrator should always keep his commitments and make certain that the teacher keeps his.

SUMMARY

The rationale for appraising the performance of school personnel is: (1) to improve performance; (2) to maintain systematic appraisal programs; (3) to keep the teacher informed as to what is expected of him; (4) to assess performance in relation to results expected; (5) to improve personal development of teachers; (6) to enable the teacher to determine for himself where fault lies for lack of performance; (7) to enable the teacher to enlighten the administrator on some points concerning performance; (8) to enable the teacher to develop on the job; (9) to provide counseling opportunities, resources and time for the teacher's personal development; (10) to enable the administrator to assist the teacher in achieving objectives.

The purposes of the post-appraisal conference are: (1) guidance and direction for setting objectives; (2) negotiating objectives; (3) problem solving.

The post-appraisal conference is a meeting between two or more individuals for the purpose of presenting and explaining essential information about the job requirement, discussing and pooling ideas and arriving at recommendations for solving problems, setting objectives, developing action plans and improving performance.

There are two types of conferences: the directed conference is for solving problems. The non-directed conference is for guidance and direction of setting objectives and for reviewing performance.

Some of the pitfalls to avoid when appraising and counseling are: (1) overcoming natural biases of administrator; (2) evaluating characteristics and traits; (3) reaching an agreement on definition of each characteristic and trait; (4) deciding on which characteristics and traits are to be appraised; (5) concentrating on performance in relation to results.

When conducting the conference, the administrator should keep the teacher or group on the subject, keep it moving, be patient, be a good listener, jot down important comments, summarize important details and avoid dictatorship, manipulation, talking too much, displaying bias, and resorting to "I suppose you would agree . . ." or "I disagree with you . . .".

The manner in which the administrator asks questions will greatly influence how they will be received. Functional questions are interrogative statements which do not get "acceptable" solutions to problems. Non-functional questions are interrogative statements which do not get "acceptable" solutions to problems.

The preliminary steps before the conference are: (1) review all essentials; (2) plan for the conference; (3) notify the teacher about the conference; (4) prepare the setting for the conference.

The administrator should prepare for the post-appraisal conference. Conducting the appraisal conference should involve: (1) reviewing the teacher's performance; (2) encouraging the teacher to do most of the talking; (3) discussing pertinent information on specific objectives; (4) taking notes; (5) making three copies of performance review statement.

The administrator should conduct the conference by summarizing or request that the teacher summarize the main points mutually agreed to in the conference. No conference is complete unless an effort is made to follow-up on the activities and recommendations made during the conference.

TEN

Motivation and Perception and Their Implications for Improving Performance

Motivating educators does not involve directly stimulating them to effective effort; of greater importance are ways of removing conditions which make teachers and administrators dissatisfied with their performance. When an educator believes in, and understands, what must be achieved, and when he is inspired to use his highest professional skill and ability to perform what he is really interested in, then—and only then—will he exert the required effort to perform well on the job. Administrators must, therefore, recognize that the only way to get a teacher to perform anything efficiently is to make him want to do it—to help him become motivated.

Each teacher and administrator has his own zone of acceptance. Performance requirements falling within this zone will be achieved with a minimum of problems. However, performance requirements which fall outside of this zone will be achieved carelessly, dishonestly or even sabotaged. The real role of the administrator is to enlarge this zone, and it is at this task of enlarging educators' acceptance to perform well that this chapter is written. The author will discuss the significance of personal goals to performance, explain the two basic categories of needs which arise from personal goals, mention how perception plays an important part in performing well, summarize some important behavioral theories related to motivation and state some signs to observe for developing motivation.

IDENTIFYING THE SIGNIFICANCE OF PERSONAL GOALS TO PERFORMANCE

Whenever an educator is deciding to accept and to take a particular course of action or to achieve an objective proposed to him, he unconsciously examines it to determine whether or not it will fulfill his own personal goals as well as those of the school system.

The administrator who feels that the teacher should be interested solely in fulfilling school goals is simply ignorant of the fact or refusing to face the fact. There is absolutely nothing unethical or unprofessional in a teacher or administrator working for his own personal goals. It is largely the responsibility of the administrator to ensure that the teacher's goals are integrated with school goals. Both goals should be taken into consideration when an administrator attempts to motivate a teacher to perform well on the job.

Charles L. Hughes says at this point:

> The integration of school goals and personal goals does not mean that teachers or administrators must adopt school goals as a replacement or exclusion of their own. It is also incorrect to assume that the sums of a teacher or administrator's goals will equal the school objectives. These assumptions have frequently posed and continue to pose problems and conflicts between teachers and administrators with each leading away from fulfilling either.[1]

Hughes states that the challenge to administrators in goal setting:

> . . . is to provide a goal setting umbrella where personal targets can be sighted and reached by individuals at all levels of the organization. This is the key to motivation at work and management must recast its concept of organization goals in this perspective—integrate the goals of the organization with the goals of its members and make personal goals attainable within the organizational framework.
>
> Humanism is not the only consideration behind such a concept. Clearly, people will seek to satisfy their personal motivation needs. So, if administration—

---

[1] Charles L. Hughes, *Goal Setting, Key to Individual Organizational Effectiveness*, American Management Association, New York, N.Y., 1965, p. 22.

1. makes *school* goals known to the employees, and
2. provides opportunities for employees to participate meaningfully in meeting their objectives,
3. in a way that gives employers a chance for identifying personal
   goals,
4. the motivation to work that results will achieve:

   a. *school* goals, as well as
   b. personal goals.[2]

The insensitive and most often the ineffective administrators fail
to perceive teachers as having personal needs and goals because quite
often they do not understand their own personal needs and goals.
They are usually those administrators who are not effective in tapping
the human potentialities of their teachers. They usually revert to restric-
tions, threats of punishments, coercion, and psychological distance
to control the behavior of their teachers which produces interpersonal
conflict within the school organization.

The sensitive and effective administrators on the other hand are
aware of their own needs and goals and thus recognize those of their
staff members. Because they are administrators who are capable of
getting the most from their teachers through mutual trust and support,
general communication, accepting conflicts as normal and working
them through, and respect for individual differences. These administrators are actively striving toward goal fulfillment and are effective
in aiding teachers to reach their own personal goals. At the same
time, they are able to achieve the higher organizational goals of the
school system.

MAINTENANCE NEEDS OF EDUCATORS: A PREREQUISITE FOR MOTIVATION

All educators need to be maintained as buildings and machines
must be maintained. The maintenance needs of teachers and administrators in schools are quite similar to an individual who is a custodian,
a secretary or a part-time bus driver. Although the maintenance of
educators is not the most important factor for motivating them to
improve their performance in the school system, it is in most cases

---

[2] *Ibid.* The author has substituted the word *school* for *company, teacher* or *administrator*
for *employees* and *administrators,* and *teachers* for *management* and *management employees*
from the original text of Charles L. Hughes.

a prerequisite for motivation. The same needs also apply to persons outside of the school, such as housewives, policemen, firemen, accountants, lawyers, etc. All must have satisfied their maintenance needs in terms of economic security, orientation, status, social and physical factors.[3] In states where collective bargaining is mandated between the board of education and the teachers' organization, most maintenance needs are usually covered in the negotiated contract.

Economic maintenance needs are salaries and fringe benefits such as teachers' retirement system, hospitalization, etc., received automatically simply by being employed in the school system. Economic maintenance needs do not include merit pay which may result from outstanding performance.

Security maintenance needs refer to the feelings of the teachers arising primarily from their perception of their individual supervisors (principal or assistant principal) as an "impartial, consistent, reassuring, friendly type of administrator." This need also results from the teachers' and administrators' knowledge that they have job protection in terms of a just system for operating the schools.

Orientation maintenance needs require that teachers and administrators receive information about the system. This information is disseminated by the administrator, school newsletters, administrative memos, policies and procedures, and information received through feedback and the "grapevine."

Status maintenance needs are usually satisfied through job descriptions, furnishings, privileges, relationships and the school's image.

Social maintenance needs are satisfied through formal and informal group discussions, preparation periods, free periods, luncheon groups or after-school recreational activities.

Physical maintenance needs are satisfied through the layout of the school building, parking facilities, teachers' rooms, air-conditioning, lighting, heat, toilet facilities, cafeteria services, noise level, smoking and other physical factors.

[3] M. Scott Myers, *Every Employee a Manager*, McGraw-Hill Book Co., New York, N.Y., 1970, pp. 11-13.

Maintenance needs are not very useful for motivating teachers and administrators to improving their performance. For example, when a teacher has been assigned to cover a class during his free period over a period of weeks and the free period is finally restored, the enthusiasm displayed by the teacher may seem to have been motivated. However, this enthusiasm soon diminishes to a level that could only be described as an absence of dissatisfaction over the loss of the free period. Initially, when the teacher was told to cover the class, the dissatisfaction was not great; however, when later informed that he would be assigned to cover the class during his free period for several weeks until a competent teacher could be hired, the dissatisfaction grew greater and greater, producing vociferous complaints. When the free period was restored to the teacher, he was not motivated; he merely returned to the level of absence of dissatisfaction. Maintenance factors are characterized by the fact that they produce very little motivation when available, but in their absence they create strong negative reactions.

M. Scott Myers states:

> Maintenance factors are peripheral to the job as they are more directly related to the environment than to work itself. For the most part, they are group administered, usually by staff personnel, and their success usually depends upon their being applied uniformly and equitably.[4]

When teachers' unions and associations gain more for their members in terms of maintenance needs, the teachers eventually fail to experience the satisfaction previously derived from these needs. They begin to make greater demands and experience more frustration in their quest for additional gains. As more maintenance needs are acquired, the opportunities for experiencing frustration increase proportionately.

Maintenance needs are important factors for fulfilling the essential personal goals of educators, but of themselves they are not factors that motivate either teachers or administrators to improve performance. Maintenance needs are prerequisites for motivation. This brings us to the second category of needs arising from personal goals; these needs are identified as motivational needs.

---

[4] *Ibid.*

MOTIVATIONAL NEEDS FOR IMPROVING PERFORMANCE

Educators have motivational needs in terms of such factors as growth, achievement, responsibility and recognition.

Growth refers to mental growth. Mental growth in the realm of education would involve: (1) Keeping up with new techniques and methods; (2) Improving teaching or administrative competence; (3) Adapting to changing practices and values; (4) Maintaining physical fitness; (5) Overcoming inflexibility through aging. One of the most important methods of motivating through mental growth is through an innovative school system which provides challenging situations for the professional staff.

Achievement refers to the need for achievement by educators. Teachers and administrators differ in terms of their need for achievement. A teacher or administrator's level of motivation will vary with his opportunity to find expression for it. In a rigid traditional school system, there may be very little opportunity for achievement; therefore, the school will most likely attract low-achieving people. An innovative school system with a reputation for doing some exciting things would most likely be attractive for high-achieving educators. School systems that attract low-achieving educators are usually satisfied primarily through the maintenance factors.

Responsibility refers to a sense of commitment to performing well in the school system. Administrators tend to have a higher sense of responsibility for performing than teachers. This is primarily because a sense of responsibility is a function of level in the organization. The superintendent assumes more responsibility than the classroom teacher. In fact, salaries are predicated on the amount of responsibility which comes with the position. However, it is also true that motivation through responsibility can also be brought about by the leadership style of the administrator. An administrator whose style of leadership is primarily autocratic will restrict the extent to which educators assume responsibilities for various tasks. On the other hand, the administrator who practices the participating decision-making process by involving his staff in the affairs that affect them, will most likely assume added responsibility in terms of job achievements.

Recognition refers to the recognition an educator earns from outstanding service. Recognition as a positive feedback is a reinforcement for motivating educators for improving performance. Recognition is at its highest point in motivating behavior when it comes from the person himself. For example, when a third grade teacher increased the number of students reading on grade level in her class from four to twenty-two, the progression of successes recognized by the teacher was the primary motivating factor. Scott Myers states, "Ideally recognition should not depend on an intermediary, but should be a natural expression of feedback from achievement itself." [5]

Once teachers and administrators have found ways to fulfill their needs adequately, their personal goals are likely to be cumulative. These goals vary with the individual and the opportunities, capacities and purposes for achievement will determine how far each person will proceed towards achieving them. All of this will be reflected in their attitudes and behavior and must be taken into account when forming a sound basis for motivation. The real problem to which this chapter is directed is to identify the current personal goals of a particular teacher or administrator. What drives or motivates one educator may leave another educator unmoved. Only when an administrator is able to visualize the aspirations (personal goals) of all of his staff members, can he be said to be in a strong position to make motivating decisions. This visualization is worth some attention because when the administration proposes a course of action which affects several teachers, they will, in turn, first determine the extent to which the action coincides with their personal goals. If the action fits, the act is most likely to be achieved; if it does not, some persuasion and incentive may be needed (motivation application).

The effective administrator will make it a point to imagine himself to be the teacher, to assess the proposed act from the teacher's point of view, to determine what the teacher's personal goals might be and to what extent they can be fulfilled. This means that the administrator must interact with each teacher individually—listening to the points of view he expresses and observing his reactions to the behavior

---

[5] *Ibid.*, p. 15.

of his peers. In this way, a good deal of information can be secured about the personal goals of the teachers.

PERCEPTION AND ITS IMPLICATIONS IN PERFORMANCE

Perception for our purposes is identified as the understanding or view that educators have of their environment. A teacher's perception of a thing, a fact or an act may be quite different from that which is real or may be different from the perception his peers may have of a thing, a fact or an act. Thus, administrators must understand the differentiation between perception and reality. For this reason, perception is extremely important to understanding human effectiveness and organizational behavior because both teachers and administrators perform on the basis of what they think (perception). Howard J. Leavitt makes this point very clear when he states:

> If one's concern as a supervisor or counselor or committee member is to try to effect some change in the behavior or performance of other people, and if in turn people's present behavior is determined largely by their perceptions of the environment, then it is critical that we seek to understand their perceptions if one is to understand the circumstances under which their behavior might change.[6]

One of the things that an educator perceives is himself (or herself) and other people. In order to protect and enhance himself, the educator may try to manipulate the picture others may have of him by presenting a front that will make his peers think what he wants them to think.

The problem revolves around how successfully the educator is able to get his act across to others. Success depends heavily on ability to pick up reactions accurately in view of the fact that accurate reactions are hard to judge because all individuals are perceiving too.

If educators act on their perceptions and different educators perceive things differently, how is the administrator to know what to expect? More specifically, what factors determine how educators will perceive

---

[6] Howard J. Leavitt, *Managerial Psychology*, The University of Chicago Press, Chicago, Ill., 1964, p. 35.

particular things, facts or acts? Human beings' perceptions are determined by the following factors:

Needs

The most important determinant of an educator's needs is his view of the world. Things that help to satisfy his needs are quickly "captured." However, things that appear to be obstacles, if they don't threaten security, may also be quickly "captured" only to be denied later on, so that it may appear to the educator that they have not appeared at all. Educators "protect" themselves, but only temporarily, by denying obstacles. If, however, the obstacle threatens security, educators are quick to face up to the reality of the real world. This is the one moment in which there exists no gap between the real and the perceived world.

Stress

The society in which we live evokes from us a number of reactions, some of which can be classified as stress situations. (A word which can be paralleled with stress is strain.) It appears that educators under stress form their perceptions and conceptions more quickly than those under less pressure.

Group Pressure

This particular concept involves a teacher who is in a situation and begins to realize that the way that he perceives a particular idea or set of circumstances is different from the rest of the professional staff. It is important to notice the influence of support from other staff members. Perhaps a key idea in understanding this particular predicament is to remember the pressures that society places on individuals who do not conform.

With reference to specific opinions that a teacher might have, an educator is more likely to retain his "objectionable" idea if the situation pertains to a concrete idea as opposed to an ambiguous one. The more nebulous the situation becomes, the more the teacher begins to question his own judgment, or for that matter, even alter his perception of the situation.

Role

How we perceive an educator depends on what we expect of that person in a given situation, which in turn depends on the role we see him fulfilling. Our society is based on certain nomenclatures given to particular people, i.e., you have children—you are a mother or a father; you administer instruction in a classroom on a daily basis—you are a teacher. Each of these titles connotes a certain manner in which that particular individual is expected to act.

During the course of a day, we all probably fill a number of different roles, although we are basically the same person in each role. As we move from one role to another, people expect different things from us and we usually fulfill their expectations. It would stand to reason then, that our behavior is greatly influenced by how we perceive ourselves in a given situation.

Reference Groups

A good number of people's ideas and attitudes are related to one or more groups. Educators use groups in a number of ways to clarify or guide their perceptions. If a teacher should see a group of children shabbily dressed, he can then look at his own children's attire in a more favorable light and see how much better he is doing than someone else. This teacher is then using another group as a reference to ascertain his present position.

Basically there are two types of relationships that an educator may have with his reference groups—normative and comparative.

Normative. When an educator uses guidelines, values and ideas of a group to gain acceptance into their organization and uses these particular values, ideas and guidelines to direct him in his thinking, he is using the normative function of reference groups.

Comparative. A teacher may again see a group of children shabbily dressed and may say to himself that although his children do not wear very expensive clothes, they are adequately dressed. In this situation, the teacher is using the group as a reference to evaluate himself.

Organizational Position

The position which an educator occupies in the school organization has a marked influence on the way that he perceives the workings of that organization.

For example, the hierarchy of a school system may include the chief school officer, his assistant, director of personnel, business manager, director of curriculum and instruction, director of pupil personnel services, principals and teachers. If a problem within the school structure were presented to them, each would view the underlying cause of the problem as different depending on his or her position.

Reward Systems

The impact of a system of rewards on a school organization is very noticeable. At least two different effects are evident.

First, there are some rewards which are directly related to the new idea development. The educator does not necessarily have to utilize the idea—only produce it.

The second noticeable impact is a production incentive. Here the educator regards the outcome of his actions in a more restricted way. Under the production incentive system, educators will more likely be concerned with the consequences of their actions.

IDENTIFYING BEHAVIORAL THEORIES

The author will not attempt to make an extensive presentation of various theories of business effectiveness and will not espouse one theory over another, but will merely cite some important behavioral theories which have received a good deal of attention for the past ten years and demonstrate their commonalities. The most appropriate theory to be used at a given time when coaching and counseling a teacher will depend on the situation and the effectiveness of the administrator in applying the theory.

THEORY X AND Y

Douglas McGregor's classic theory identifies two assumptions about human beings. His Theory X assumes that people need authority and coercion to motivate them to perform on the job, that satisfactory performance can only come about through facing, ordering and forbidding. This theory further maintains that most people avoid work or responsibility, that they need precise directions for achieving objectives and that they must be tightly controlled and will abuse freedom. Theory X holds that people must be rewarded for their success and punished for their lack or nonperformance. Theory Y assumes that people prefer to discipline themselves through self-direction and self-control, that people will react better to challenges than to authority, and that they will seek responsibility and can enjoy work. McGregor's Theory further assumes that high expectations and frequent opportunities make it possible to set meaningful goals which result in high performance. Theory Y is the foundation for school management by objectives.[7]

HUMAN ORGANIZATION THEORY

Rensis Likert has identified four systems of managerial style. System 1 is the exploitive authentic style by which human effectiveness is controlled by authority and coercion, without regard to the needs of the human being. System 1 is still prominent in most school districts in the country. System 2 is the benevolent authoritative style, which considers the needs of the human being. System 2 is an outgrowth of System 1 which provides some improvement in performance but also some paternalism. System 3, the consultative style, is that human beings are consulted when they are called on to perform, but this system leads to the manipulation of people and the continuation of management prerogatives of accepting a rejected suggestion offered by the employee. System 4, the participation style, is the ideal model. Here the talent and competence of individual employees will effectively achieve organizational goals if they have access to information and are involved in solving problems and achieving their own goals.[8]

Obviously, System 4 describes school management by objectives and the objectives-centered approach to performance appraisal.

---

[7] Douglas McGregor, *The Professional Manager*, McGraw-Hill Book Co., New York, N.Y., 1967.

[8] Rensis Likert, *The Human Organization*. McGraw-Hill Book Co., New York, N.Y., 1967.

HIERARCHY OF NEEDS THEORY

Abraham H. Maslow's theory identifies motivation "as having an internal motive that incites an individual to perform some kind of action." Maslow maintains that motivation comes from within the individual and cannot be imposed on him. To Maslow, man is seen as a goal seeker from the beginning of his life to his death. The action an individual takes to reach a goal is his drive and the acting out of a drive is the result of motivation to achieve the goal. This process is converted to a set of needs identified as Maslow's Hierarchy of Needs:

- Physiological Needs
  - Safety Needs
    - Need for Belongingness and Love
      - Need for Esteem
        - Need for Self-Actualization

Maslow maintains that unless the basic needs are satisfied, such as physiological needs and safety needs, the succeeding need cannot be satisfied. For example, if an educator's job is in jeopardy, he may be willing to risk his safety to maintain his physiological needs.[9]

MOTIVATION—HYGIENE THEORY

Frederick Herzberg theorizes that the focus of motivation should be on the self-fulfilling, achievement-motivated, self-actualizing needs of employees. He maintains that job enrichment should be the motivated work force. Job enrichment is referred to the challenging content of the job, that will cause the employee to grow both in skills and techniques and in improving his relationship and attitudes about his job. Meaningless tasks which offer very little opportunity for self-expression of talent may result in hygiene seeking (lower order needs); however, on the other hand, meaningful work which offers opportunity

---

[9] Abraham H. Maslow, *Toward a Psychology of Being*, 2nd ed., Van Nostrand Co., Inc., New York, N.Y., 1968.

for self-expression, growth, advancement, latent responsibility, achievement and recognition produces motivation and tends to de-emphasize a person's hygienic needs.[10]

INDIVIDUAL AND ORGANIZATION GOALS THEORY

Chris Argyris' theory maintains that human beings cannot be motivated, but are by nature motivated. He indicates that the problem of the organization is the direction and form the motivation by nature takes. He asserts that human beings possess "psychological energy" and that it is used in one form or another. Because human needs are more important than any other need, personal goals take precedence over organizational goals. If the person perceives that organizational goals are placed before his personal goals, then psychological energy may be directed towards tension, conflict, dissatisfaction and subversion over the organizational objectives.[11]

POWER STRUCTURE THEORY

John Pare's power structure defines human effectiveness as related to sources of power. He identifies four forms of power. Boss power is expressed as the authority controlled relationship or the use of authority in relation to level or status. Boss power is sometimes expressed as "management power" or "system power" imposed through the controls of management systems, procedures and policies. Peer power is brought about due to the influence of co-workers' emphasis of group goals and needs over the goals and needs of the organization. Goal power refers to generated action emanating from meaningful goals which satisfy individual and organizational needs.[12]

ORGANIZATIONAL GOVERNING SYSTEMS THEORY

Warren Bennis' theory maintains that bureaucracy tends to reduce human initiative through its complex network of inflexible restrictive rules and systems. He further states, however, that democracy is inevit-

---

[10] Frederick Herzberg, *Work and the Nature of Man*, The World Publishing Co., Cleveland, Ohio, 1966.

[11] Chris Argyris, *Integrating the Individual and the Organization*, John Wiley & Sons, Inc., New York, N.Y., 1964.

[12] John Pare, *What's Your Power Structure?*, Canadian Business, April, 1968.

able for the successful operation of the organization because it gives people an opportunity to express themselves in defining and achieving personal organizational goals in a flexible, adoptive and supervisory goal-oriented climate.[13]

There are no fixed or standard solutions to human effectiveness. There are, however, some guidelines to effective motivation; that is, there are some recommendations which may help to facilitate the motivation of educators in the performance of their professional responsibility. These guidelines are as follows:

1. Establish a resource of knowledge of human behavioral theories and be able to apply them intelligently.
2. Constantly analyze and become aware of the individual needs of staff members and the ever-changing circumstances and conditions which affect motivation and the achievement of objectives.
3. Communicate the goals and objectives of the school system and state what the educators can expect from the school in terms of a career.
4. Demonstrate sincerity and integrity in carrying out personnel policies which are intended to attract, select, hire, train, motivate, reward and retain competent professional staff members.
5. Be flexible in the management of human beings.

OBSERVING SIGNS FOR APPLYING MOTIVATIONAL THEORIES

Once the administrator has gained some knowledge about motivational theories, he can begin to look for signs that indicate the direction for applying motivation. The following are some illustrations:

1. Is the teacher seeking appreciation and recognition?
   Does he frequently visit the school office?
   Does he take a front seat at faculty meetings?
   Does he remember and repeat complimentary things said about him?
   Does he go out of his way to do things for members of the staff?
   Does he stop the principal in the hall to report about a job he did perform well?

---

[13] Warren Bennis, *Changing Organizations*, McGraw-Hill Book Co., New York, N.Y., 1966.

2. Does the teacher attach great importance to comfort and good working conditions? The following questions should be considered:
Does he constantly recommend better layouts, more convenient handling of school matters?
Does he keep his teacher aide busy with non-professional chores?
Does he keep his desk and classroom orderly?
Does he often attempt to smooth over disagreements between teachers?

3. Does the teacher thrive on the companionship of other teachers? The following questions should be helpful:
Does he obviously value his family relationship?
Does he talk about his wife, children and relatives at great lengths?
Does he work but with small groups?
Does he join professional associations, clubs, churches, political parties, and actively participate in their affairs?
Does he continue close friendships?

4. Does the teacher seek information and want to be in the know? These are some of the questions which should be considered:
Does he try anything at least once?
Does he read much?
Does he take college courses even though he is certified in his teaching?
Does he enroll in inservice courses?
Does he continually ask questions?

5. Does the teacher enjoy a feeling of accomplishment? The following questions might be helpful:
Does he frequent the principal's office to suggest promotions for himself?
Does he worry about bills?
Does he apply for home tutoring to gain more compensation?
Does he actively participate in negotiating sessions seeking more money and fringe benefits?
Does he donate to worthy causes?

6. Is the teacher seeking status? The following questions would be helpful in determining this:
Does he seek promotion at the same salary?
Does he run for office in teachers' local and-or state associations?

Does he actively participate in community affairs?

Does he attempt to meet more than the normal requirements for his position?

7. Does the teacher thrive on responsibility? The following questions would help:

Does he report to school on time?

Does he accept blame when things go wrong?

Does he use up all of his yearly accumulation of sick days?

Does he work well on his own when not being observed?

Does he seek and take on jobs for which he knows others will hold him accountable?

8. Is the teacher in search of security? The following might give some indications:

Does he keep his classroom locked at all times?

Does he contribute the greatest amount possible to the retirement system?

Does he observe and obey all safety rules and regulations?

Does he guard his health carefully?

The clue to motivating an educator often lies in a host of comparatively trivial things and it will pay the administrator to observe them and try to understand what they mean. The administrator should:

1. Note the things spoken and done by the teacher on and off the job; when things go right or wrong; when performing by himself or with others.

2. Avoid jumping to conclusions about the teacher; that he is careful or sloppy; looking at what he does—that is the only criteria of what he may or may not be.

3. Continue to observe the teacher even after there is evidence as to his personal goals. He will also have other needs which must be fulfilled.

4. Do not waste time in deciding whether the teacher is right or wrong in what he wants. The administrator's job is to integrate the teacher's personal goals with the school's goals.

SUMMARY

The important task of an administrator is to integrate the teacher's personal goals with those of the school system. There are two categories of needs. The first, which is a prerequisite for the second, is maintenance needs. These needs are: economic security, orientation, status, social and physical.

The second category of needs are motivational needs. These needs are growth, achievement, responsibility and recognition. Perception is identified as the understanding educators have of things in the environment around them. Perception may be influenced by needs, stress, group pressure, role reference groups, organizational positions and reward systems. There are several behavioral theories; however, no one theory can be supported over another. The effectiveness of the theories depends upon the situation and the person applying them. The administrator must remain alert to detect signs which point the way for motivating.

APPENDIX

Administering Policy and Procedure Statement for Implementing School Management by Objectives

SCHOOL MANAGEMENT BY OBJECTIVES

(Ensuring Educational Accountability)

Wyandanch Public Schools
Wyandanch, New York

This is an administrative policy and procedure statement issued by the chief school officer to guide all professional personnel in the Wyandanch School District in setting up specific performance objectives and action plans. Performance objectives for central administration staff, supervisors, principals, and assistant principals are developed before those of the staff. The performance objective and action plans for each school, for the central administration staff and for the sub-divisions will serve as the individual charter of educational accountability. The combined charters will serve as the School District's Charter of Educational Accountability.

GENERAL POLICY

It is an administrative policy of the Wyandanch School District that performance objectives are to be used in all school organizational units (buildings, teams, departments, and sub-divisions) and by all professional staff members. However, the specific procedure may vary from unit to unit. All short-range performance objectives should be on a school year. Long-range goals are usually projected over a period of three years or more.

DEFINITION

"School management by objectives" refers to an administrative and supervisory method whereby educators develop and establish goals for their professional job at the beginning of each school year. School management by objectives is not an addition to an administrator's, supervisor's, or teacher's job; it is a means to improve their performance on the job. Performance objectives should not only include professional skill objectives but should also include goals of a creative nature, or, special or "break through" activities resulting from new technologies or to new approaches to problems. Also, objectives are to be established for personal development to improve basic skills. In all instances it is desirable to establish observable terms to measure results.

APPLICATION IN A SCHOOL

The first step in developing performance objectives in a school is to establish the specific performance objectives for the building principal (these objectives are usually based upon long range goals projected by the board of education and the chief school officer). After the objectives of a school have been drafted for the school year, the chief school officer or his assistant meet with the building principal and mutually agree to a Statement of Performance Objectives for the school year toward which the principal will direct his efforts. This Statement of Performance Objectives should be oriented toward solving the particular problems of the school and be directly related to criteria used for appraising the school's performance.

The second step is to establish a Statement of Performance Objectives for each individual reporting directly to the building principal. The procedure used is similar to that used in developing the performance objectives for the principal. Working with each of his team leaders and/or department chairman and persons in charge of a sub-division either the assistant principal or principal mutually agrees with each of them for the school year. Each performance objective should be related to the performance objectives of the principal and these to the overall objective of the school and the school district.

A similar procedure is used for all other members in the school organization unit. The performance objectives and action plans of each individual should be mutually agreed to by his immediate supervisor and should be related to the performance objectives of the immediate supervisor.

After all performance objectives and action plans have been established for administrators and supervisors reporting directly to the principal, he should review them as a group to be sure that they are compatible and constitute an integrated plan for achieving objectives of that unit.

The combined performance objectives and action plans of each team department and sub-division, supervisors and administrators will serve as the charter of educational accountability for individual schools.

APPLICATION IN CENTRAL ADMINISTRATION AND SUB-DIVISIONS

Performance objectives in the central administration and sub-divisions should be accomplished in the same way as in a school building. A Statement of Performance Objectives should be related to the objectives of school districts and to the objectives of the specific unit of the central administrative staff and sub-divisions which require the assistance of his department. Then the performance objectives and action plans for all other members in the department should be developed. All performance objectives and action plans within a particular department should be reviewed as a group so that they constitute an integrated plan for achieving the department's objectives.

TYPES OF PERFORMANCE OBJECTIVES

An individual's list of performance objectives should represent a balanced projected performance plan. The following list includes examples of educational areas that should be considered wherever applicable.

1. Professional skill objectives. This type of objective should be developed only when an individual's ordinary duties are not being performed satisfactorily.

2. Problem-solving objectives. When professional skill objectives are not being performed adequately, the need for problem-solving objectives becomes apparent. Problem-solving objectives also become a necessity when an emergency situation occurs creating a problem, such as fire, hurricane, flood, etc.

3. Innovative objectives. In order to improve on the status quo, performance objectives of a creative nature should be developed, such as the implementation of the Cureton Reading Program.

4. Personal development objectives. This type of objective is set in order to improve the basic professional skills of an educator. Usually when innovative objectives are set, personal development objectives follow.

PROPER STATEMENT OF PERFORMANCE OBJECTIVES

Because of the major importance of the school management by objectives program, it is necessary that great care be given to the preparation of Statement of Performance Objectives and action plans. The following guides are recommended:

1. A professional skill basic criteria guide should be developed for administrators and teachers. This guide is to be used as the basis for assessing appropriate performance and professional skill areas needing improvement. The items assessed "needs improvement" are used for setting professional skill objectives.

2. At least one problem-solving objective, two innovative objectives and two personal development objectives should be established for each administrator and supervisor. All teams and departments will establish at least one problem-solving objective and two innovative objectives. Each member of a team or department must individually set two personal development objectives.

3. All objectives are to include the three basic components which are, the condition, the act, and the minimal level of acceptable performance. In addition, all objectives must include an action plan for

meeting the objective. All performance objectives and action plans should be included in a Statement of Performance Objectives which would include the name and title of the person submitting the Statement, the name and title of his immediate supervisor. All Statements must contain the signature of the person submitting the statement and his immediate supervisor.

4. The objectives should define reasonably attainable, but challenging goals; that is, they must represent relatively optimistic goals, the accomplishment of which will contribute significantly to attainment of the broad educational and school building goals.

5. They should be stated in such a way that their performance can be clearly measured. This requires the use of precise and understandable terms, such as to increase, to implement, to compare, etc.

6. The statement should include, when applicable, both quantitative (how much) and qualitative (how well) objectives. Whenever qualitative objectives are set, minimal level of successful performance can be ascertained from a survey, a questionnaire, or a committee of judges.

7. Short range objectives for meeting long range goals should be included in the Statement of Performance Objectives. *Each year, the board of education will publish its long range goals.*

All school personnel are legally and professionally charged with the responsibility and accountability for setting short range objectives in order to achieve the long range goals set by the board of education.

ADMINISTRATION DURING THE SCHOOL YEAR

Each performance objective and action plan is a tool for the use of the educator and his immediate supervisor. Both should have copies of the individual's Statement of Performance Objectives for ready reference. During the course of the school year conditions can change and thus affect the performance objectives. When this happens the performance objectives and action plan should be modified by the individual educator and his immediate supervisor. Compensating changes may also be required in the performance objectives and action plan for other individuals so that the achievement of all performance objectives will still result in the achievement of the objectives of the school organizational unit. *However, care must be exercised to avoid*

*continually changing performance objectives which may cause perfor-
mance objectives to lose their significance.*

Maximum benefit can be obtained by making the performance objectives and action plan the basis of regular performance appraisal review
and by coaching and counseling throughout the school year with the
individual concerned. Such reviews yield two beneficial results: the
administrator or supervisor can more effectively coordinate the efforts
of the members of his staff, and the staff members can obtain advice
and guidance on his action plans for achieving his specific performance
objectives.

REVIEW OF OBJECTIVES

A. Team leaders, department chairman reporting to assistant principals or principals.

1. Check monthly on objectives scheduled for completion the
previous month. Follow specific objectives as required.

2. Evaluate progress on all objectives quarterly and report progress to assistant principal or principal.

3. Prepare periodic review of performance (Performance
Appraisal Review form) and informally confer with assistant principal
or principal.

4. Prepare written evaluation of performance on all objectives
using Performance Appraisal Review form quarterly. Submit report
to assistant principal or principal within two weeks after each quarter
of the school year.

B. Principals, directors, supervisors, and all central administrative
professional personnel.

1. During the school year on a quarterly basis, check progress
on objectives and informally review with immediate supervisors.

2. Prepare written evaluation of performance on all objectives
using Performance Appraisal Review form. Submit report to administrative assistant and chief school officer within two weeks after each
quarter of the school year.

James Lewis, Jr.
District Principal
July 1, 1972

BIBLIOGRAPHY

Almy, H. C., and Herbert Sorenson. *Almy-Sorenson Rating Scale for Teachers*. Bloomington, Ill.: Public Schools Publishing Company (not dated).

American Educational Research Association. "Teacher Personnel," *Review of Educational Research*, XIX, No. 3 (June, 1949), 175-276.

———. "Teacher Personnel," *Review of Educational Research*, XXV, No. 3 (June, 1955), 189-275.

———. "Teachers and Non-Academic Personnel," *Review of Educational Research*, XXII, No. e (June, 1952), 163-271.

Anderson, C. C., and S. M. Hunka. "Teacher Evaluation: Some Problems and a Proposal," *Harvard Educational Review*, XXXIII, No. 1 (1963), 74-96.

Anderson, H. H., J. E. Brewer, and M. F. Reed. "Studies of Teachers' Classroom Personalities"; Follow-up studies of the effects of dominative and integrative contacts on children's behavior; *Applied Psychology Monograph*, III, No. 11 (1946).

Argyris, Chris. *Integrating The Individual and The Organization*. New York, N.Y.: John Wiley & Sons, Inc. (1964).

Asch, S. E. "Effects of Group Pressure upon the Modification and Distortion of Judgments"; In E. E. Maccoby, M. M. Newcomb, and E. L. Hartley (eds.), *Readings in Social Psychology*. New York: Henry Holt and Co. (1958).

203

Ashman, M. "Teachers in Summit, N.J. Say Merit Pay Works," *School Management,* Vol. IV, No. 4 (April, 1960), 69-73, 142, 144-145.

Association for Supervision and Curriculum Development, NEA. *Better Than Rating.* Washington, D. C.: (1950).

Baughman, M. D., W. Anderson, M. Smith, and E. Wiltse, *Administration and Supervision of the Modern Secondary School.* West Nyack, N.Y.: Parker Publishing Company (1969).

Beck, Samuel J. *Rorschach's Test: I, Basic Processes.* 2nd ed. New York: Grune and Stratton, Inc., (1949).

Beecher, Dwight E. *The Evaluation of Teaching: Backgrounds and Concepts.* Syracuse, N.Y.: Syracuse University Press (1949).

—————. *The Teaching Evaluation Record.* Buffalo: Educators Publishing Company (1953).

Bennis, Warren. *Changing Organizations.* New York, N.Y.: McGraw-Hill Book Co. (1966).

Biddle, B. J. "The Integration of Teacher Effectiveness Research," *Contemporary Research on Teacher Effectiveness.* New York: Holt, Rinehart and Winston, Inc. (1964), 1-40.

Boardman, C. W., H. R. Douglass and R. K. Bent. *Democratic Supervision in Secondary Schools.* Boston: Houghton Mifflin Company (1953), Chs. X, XXI.

Bradford, E., A. Doremus, and C. Kreismer, *Elementary School Evaluation: Administrator's Guide to Accountability.* West Nyack, N.Y.: Parker Publishing Company (1972).

Brain, George B. and Thomas C. Pullen, Jr. *Increasing Your Administrative Skills in Dealing with the Instructional Program.* Englewood Cliffs, N.J.: Prentice-Hall, Inc. (1966).

Brickman, Benjamin. "Rewarding the Superior Teacher," *School and Society,* Vol. 77. (September, 1959), 356-358.

Brownell, William A. "The Mission of Colleges for Teacher Education in Insuring Quality of Classroom Instruction," address to annual meeting of American Association of Colleges for Teacher Education. Chicago (1957).

Bruner, J. S. *On Knowing.* Cambridge: Harvard University Press (1962).

Bruner, J. S. and R. Tagiuri. "The Perceptions of People," in G. Lindzey (ed.) *Handbook of Social Psychology*. Cambridge: Addison-Wesley Publishing Co., Inc. (1954), 634-654.

Burton, W. H. and L. J. Brueckner. *Supervision; a Social Process*. New York: Appleton-Century-Crofts, Inc. (1955), 356-358.

Bush, Robert Nelson. *The Teacher-Pupil Relationship*. Englewood Cliffs, N.J.: Prentice-Hall, Inc. (1954).

California Journal of Secondary Education, Vol. XXXV has a comprehensive symposium on "The Constructive Use of Teacher Talents," (team teaching). (April, 1960), 232-270.

Callahan, M., *The Effective School Department Head*, West Nyack, N.Y.: Parker Publishing Company (1971).

Cantril, Hadley. *The Why of Man's Experience*. New York: The Macmillan Company (1950).

Chandler, B. J. "Merit Rating Not Detrimental to Morale," *The Nation's Schools*, Vol. 61. (April, 1958), 58-60.

Chandler, B. J. and P. V. Petty. *Personnel Management in School Administration*. Yonkers-On-Hudson: World Book Company (1955), Ch. IX.

Charters, W. W. and Douglas Waples. *The Commonwealth Teacher-Training Study*. Chicago: The University of Chicago Press (1929).

Conant, J. B. *The Education of American Teachers*. New York: McGraw-Hill (1954).

Cook, Walter W. and Dyril J. Hoyt. "Procedure for Determining Number and Nature of Norm Groups for the Minnesota Teacher Attitude Inventory," *Educational and Psychological Measurement*, XII, No. 4. (Winter, 1952), 562-573.

Cook, Walter W., N. C. Kearney, P. D. Rocchio, and A. Thompson. "Significant Factors in Teachers' Classroom Attitudes," *Journal of Teacher Education*, VII, No. 3. (September, 1956), 274-279.

Cook, Walter W., C. H. Leeds, and R. Callis. *Minnesota Teacher Attitude Inventory Manual*. New York: Psychological Corp. (1951).

Cooperative Study of Secondary School Standards. *Evaluation*

Criteria. Washington, D. C.: American Council of Education (1950).

Crutchfield, R. S. "Conformity and Character," *American Psychologist*, 10. (1955), 191-198.

Dale, Ernest and Alice Smith. "Now Report Cards for Bosses," *New York Times Magazine*. (March 31, 1957), 25, 56, 58, 60.

Daniels, Lydia. "Teacher Perceptions on the Role of a Teacher." Unpublished Master's Thesis, University of California, Los Angeles (1964).

Drucker, Peter F. "The New Philosophy Comes to Life," *Harper's Magazine*. (August, 1957), 36-40.

Dyer, Frank. "Teacher Role Expectations of a Secondary School Staff." Unpublished Doctoral Dissertation, University of California, Los Angeles (1966).

The Education of Teachers: Certification, Official Report of the San Diego Conferences, TEPS, Washington: National Education Association (1960), 79-199 and part III.

Educational Testing Service. *The National Teacher Examinations*. Bulletin of Information. Princeton, N.J. (1957).

————. *Teacher Education Examination Program*. Handbook for Presidents, Deans, and Department Heads. Princeton, N.J. (not dated).

Edwards, Allen L. *Personal Preference Schedule*. Manual. New York: Psychological Corporation (1954).

Elsbree, W. S. and D. R. Davies. *Instructional Personnel Record*. Elsbree-Davies Personnel Record Series. New York: Bureau of Publications, Teachers College, Columbia University (1945).

Elsbree, W. S. and H. J. McNally. *Elementary School Administration and Supervision*, 2nd ed. New York: American Book Company (1959), Ch. X.

Elsbree, W. S. and E. Edmund Reutter, Jr. *Staff Personnel in the Public Schools*. Englewood Cliffs, N.J.: Prentice-Hall, Inc. (1954).

Forrester, Jay W. "Systems Analysis as a Tool for Urban Planning." Cambridge, Mass.: Massachusetts Institute of Technology (1969), (mimeographed paper) 15.

General Foods Corporation. *How Are You Doing On Your Job?* New York (1949).

Hart, J. W. *Teachers and Teaching.* New York: The Macmillan Company (1934).

Hathaway, S. R. and J. C. McKinley. *Minnesota Multiphasic Personality Inventory.* Rev. ed., Manual. New York: Psychological Corporation (1951).

Haverhill (Mass.) Public and Vocational Schools. *Evaluation Inventory.* Haverhill: The Schools (not dated).

Heath, R. W. "Curriculum, Cognition and Educational Measurement," *Journal of Education and Psychological Measurement*, 24, (2). (1964), 239-354.

Herman, W., *Principal's Guide to Teacher Personnel Problems in the Elementary School,* West Nyack, N.Y.: Parker Publishing Company (1966).

Herzberg, Frederick. *Work and the Nature of Man.* Cleveland, Ohio: The World Publishing Co. (1966).

Hicks, William V. and Marshall C. Jameson. *The Elementary School Principal at Work.* Englewood Cliffs, N.J.: Prentice-Hall, Inc. (1957).

Highet, G. *The Art of Teaching.* New York: Alfred A. Knopf, Inc. (1950).

The High School Journal, "Merit Rating," Vol. XLIII. (May, 1960), *passim.*

Huggett, A. J. and T. M. Stinnett. *Professional Problems of Teachers.* New York: The Macmillan Company (1956), Chs. II, IV-VI.

Hughes, Charles L. *Goal Setting, Key To Individual Organizational Effectiveness.* New York: American Management Association (1965).

Hutchins, R. M. *Education and Freedom.* New York: Grove Press (1963).

Information on Merit Rating, Research Bulletin No. 59-1. Raleigh,

Box 350: North Carolina Education Association (October, 1959), *passim*.

Jersild, Arthur T. *When Teachers Face Themselves*. New York: Bureau of Publications, Teachers College, Columbia University (1955).

Jones, Margaret Lois. "Analysis of Certain Aspects of Teaching Ability," *Journal of Experimental Education*, XXV, no. 2. (December, 1956), 153-180.

The Journal of Teacher Education. (June, 1957). Issue is devoted almost entirely to the subject of merit rate salary schedules for teachers.

Kaplan, J. D. "An Example of Student-Generated Sequences in Mathematics Instruction," *The Mathematics Teacher* (May, 1964).

Kay, E. and J. R. P. France, Jr. "A Study of the Performance Appraisal Interview," *Behavioral Research Service, Technical Report*. University of Michigan (1961).

Kearney, N. C. *A Teacher's Professional Guide*. Englewood Cliffs, N.J.: Prentice-Hall, Inc. (1958). Ch. IX.

Kelley, Ida B. and Keith J. Perkins. *How I Teach*. Purdue Teachers Examination, Educational Test Bureau. Minneapolis: Educational Publishers, Inc. (1942).

Killian, Ray A. *Managing by Design for Maximum Executive Effectiveness*. New York: American Management Association (1968).

Kinney, Lucien B. *Measure of A Good Teacher*. San Francisco: California Teachers Association (1953).

Kuder, G. F. *Kuder Preference Record–Vocational, Form C-H*. Chicago: Science Research Associates, Inc. (1949).

Lewin, K., R. Lippitt and R. K. White. "Patterns of Aggressive Behavior in Experimentally Created 'Social Climate'." In A. P. Colodarci (ed.), *Educational Psychology*. New York: Dryden Press (1955), 271-299.

Lewis, James Jr. *A Systems Approach to Developing Behavioral Objectives*. Wyandanch, N.Y.: Northeast Association for the Individualization of Instruction (1970).

Lieberman, Myron. *Education as a Profession*. Englewood Cliffs, N.J.: Prentice-Hall, Inc. (1956).

———. *The Future of Public Education*. Chicago: University of Chicago Press (1960), Ch. XII.

Lien, Arnold Juel. "A Comparative-Predictive Study of Students in the Four Curricula of a Teacher Education Institution," *Journal of Experimental Education*, XXI, No. 2. (December, 1952), 81-219.

Likert, Rensis. *The Human Organization*. New York: McGraw-Hill Book Co. (1967).

———. *New Patterns of Management*. New York: McGraw-Hill Book Co. (1961), 45.

Lindquist, E. F., et al. *The Iowa Tests of Educational Development*. Chicago: Science Research Associates (1948).

Maslow, Abraham H. *Toward a Psychology of Being*, 2nd Ed. New York: Van Nostrand Co. (1968).

McAnkey, Dale D. *How to Manage by Results*. New York: American Management Association (1967).

McCormick, D. P. *The Power of People*. New York: Harper & Brothers (1949).

McGregor, Douglas. *The Human Side of Enterprise*. New York: McGraw-Hill Book Co. (1960), 87.

———. *The Professional Manager*. New York: McGraw-Hill Book Co. (1967).

Medley, Donald M. and Harold E. Mitzel. "Measuring Classroom Behavior by Systematic Observation," *Handbook of Research on Teaching*, N. L. Gage Editor. Chicago: Rand McNally & Co. (1963), 247-328.

———. "Studies of Teacher Behavior: The Refinement of Two Techniques for Observing Teachers' Classroom Behaviors." New York: Division of Teacher Education, Board of Higher Education of the City of New York (October, 1955).

Medley, Donald M. and Ida F. Williams. "Predicting Teacher Effectiveness with the Minnesota Multiphasic Personality Inventory." New York: Division of Teacher Education, Board of Higher Education of the City of New York (February, 1957).

Mee, John F. "Management Philosophy for Professional Executives," *Business Horizons*, Supplement to the *Indiana Business Review* (February, 1957), 5.

Meyer, H. H., F. Kay and J. R. P. French, Jr. "Split Role In Performance Appraisal," *Harvard Business Review* (January-February, 1965), 125-126.

Misner, Paul J. "The Merit Rating Issue," *Seven Studies*. Evanston, Ill.: National School Boards Association, Inc. (1958), 42-55.

Mitzel, Harold E. and Cecily F. Gross. "A Critical Review of the Development of Pupil Growth Criteria in Studies of Teacher Effectiveness." New York: Division of Teacher Education, Board of Higher Education of the City of New York (April, 1956).

————. "Development of Pupil-Growth Criteria in Studies of Teacher Effectiveness." Part II. *Educational Research Bulletin*, 37: 205-215 (1958).

Moore, H. E. and N. B. Walters. *Personnel Administration in Education*. New York: Harper and Brothers (1955). Part II.

Morphet, Edgar L. and Charles O. Ryan. *Designing Education for the Future*, No. 3. New York: Citation Press (1967).

Morris, Elizabeth H. *Morris Trait Index L*. Bloomington, Ill.: Public School Publishing Company (not dated).

————. *Teacher's Handbook for Morris Trait Index L*. Bloomington, Ill.: Public School Publishing Company (not dated).

Morrisey, George L. *Management by Objectives and Results*. Reading, Mass.: Addison, Wesley (1970).

Myers, M. Scott. *Every Employee A Manager*. New York: McGraw-Hill Book Co. (1970).

National Commission on Teacher Education and Professional Standards. "Factors in Teaching Competence," Report of Special Group A, The Albany Conference, 1954.

————. "Measures of Teacher Competences," Report of Special Group D, The Miami Beach Conference, 1953.

National Education Association. "Status of the American Public School Teacher," *Research Bulletin*, XXXV, No. 1. Washington, D.C. (February, 1957).

————. "Teacher Personnel Practices, 1950-51: Appointment and Termination of Service," *Research Bulletin*, XXX, No. 1. Washington, D.C. (February, 1952).

National Industrial Conference Board. "Appraisal of Job Performance," Studies in Personnel Policy 121. New York (1951).

————. "Determining Salesmen's Base Pay—A Role of Job Evaluation," Studies in Personnel Policy 98. New York (1948).

————. "Evaluating Managerial Positions," Studies in Personnel Policy 122. New York (1951).

————. "Developing Management Competence: Changing Concepts and Merging Practices," Studies in Personnel Policy 189. New York (1964).

————. "Marks of the Good Worker." Reprinted from *Management Record*, XVIII, No. 5 (May, 1956).

NEA Journal, vol. L (January, 1961). Presents preliminary findings of national committee on "New Horizons in Teacher Education and Professional Standards," 55-68.

NEA Research Bulletin, Washington, presents up-to-date information on merit rating from time to time; for example "Salary Provisions for Quality of Service," vol. XXXVIII, No. 4 (December, 1959), 106-110.

NEA Research Division, Washington: *Special Memo: Quality-of-Service in Teachers' Salary Schedules* (July, 1956). A report on 556 school districts of 30,000 or more population.

Nelson, K. G., John E. Bicknell and Paul A. Hedlund. *Measures of Teaching Effectiveness*. First Report of Cooperative Study to Predict Effectiveness in Secondary School Teaching. Albany: University of the State of New York (1956).

New England School Development Council. *Teacher Competence and Its Relation to Salary*. Cambridge, Mass. (1956).

New Jersey State Department of Education. *District-Wide Improvement Program*. Trenton, N.J. (pamphlet).

Odiorne, George S. *Management by Objectives*. New York: Pitman Publishing Corp. (1965).

————. *Management by Objectives, A System of Managerial Leadership*. New York: Pitman Publishing Corp. (1965).

————. *Management Decisions by Objectives*. Englewood Cliffs, N.J.: Prentice-Hall, Inc. (1969).

————. *Personnel Administration by Objectives*. Homewood, Ill.: Richard D. Irwin, Inc. (1971).

Ohio Teaching Record. Anecdotal Observation Form, 2nd rev. ed. Columbus: College of Education, Ohio State University (1945).

Olsson, David E. *Management by Objectives*. Palo Alto, California: Pacific Books Publishers (1968).

Otis, Arthur S. *Otis Quick-Scoring Ability Tests*. Manual of Directions for Gamma Test. Yonkers-On-Hudson, N.Y.: World Book Company (1937).

Pare, John. *What's Your Power Structure?* Canadian Business (April, 1968).

Phi Delta Kappan, vol. XLII (January, 1961). Includes seven articles on merit rating and pay.

Raudsepp, Eugene. "Bridge The Gap With Questions," *Machine Design*. Cleveland, Ohio: Penton Publications (1970).

Redfern, George B. *How to Appraise Teaching Performance*. Columbus, Ohio: School Management Institute, Inc. (1963).

Redl, F. and W. W. Wattenberg. *Mental Hygiene in Teaching*. New York: Harcourt-Brace and Co. (1959).

Review of Educational Research, Vol. XXII (June, 1952), presents the first "Report of the Committee on the Criteria of Teacher Effectiveness" of the American Educational Research Association; Vol. XXV (June, 1955) brings up to date "The Measurement and Prediction of Teaching Efficiency," 261-269; and Vol. XXVIII (June, 1958) adds new research on "The Measurement and Prediction of Teaching Efficiency," 256-264.

Rogers, V. M., ed. *Merit Rating for Teachers?* Syracuse: Syracuse University Press (1959)

Ryans, D. G. *Characteristics of Teachers: Their Description, Comparison, and Appraisal*. Washington: American Council on Education (1960). *passim*.

Ryans, David G. "The Investigation of Teacher Characteristics," *The Educational Record*, XXXIV (October, 1953), 371-396.

Schleh, Edward C. *Management by Results*. New York: McGraw-Hill Book Co. (1961), p. 38.

Schwartz, Alfred and Stuart C. Tiedeman. *Evaluating Student Progress in the Secondary School*. New York: Longmans, Green & Company (1957).

Smith, E. R. and R. W. Tyler. *Appraising and Recording Student Progress*. New York and London: Harper and Brothers (1942).

Smith, J. K. "Discovery of Patterns in the Difference of Two Squares," *The Mathematics Teacher* (May, 1964).

Sorenson, A. G. "What is learned in Practice Teaching?", *Journal of Teacher Education*. In press (1966).

Sorenson, A. G., T. R. Husek and Constance Yu. "Divergent Concepts of Teacher Role: An Approach to the Measurement of Teacher Effectiveness." *Journal of Educational Psychology*, 54: 287-294 (1963).

State of Delaware. *Teacher's Rating Card*. Dover: Department of Public Instruction (not dated).

Steig, L. R., and R. K. Frederick, *School Personnel and In-Service Training Programs*, West Nyack, N.Y.: Parker Publishing Company (1969).

Stern, G. C., M. I. Stein and B. S. Bloom. *Methods in Personality Assessment*. Glencoe, Ill.: The Free Press (1951).

Strong, E. K., Jr. *Vocational Interest Blank for Men*. Rev. ed. Palo Alto, California: Stanford University Press (1951).

Taba, Hilda and Elizabeth Noel. *Action Research: A Case Study*. Washington, D. C.: Association for Supervision and Curriculum Development, NEA (1957).

Tagiuri, R. and L. Petrullo (eds.). *Person Perception and Interpersonal Behavior*. Stanford: Stanford University Press (1958).

Teacher Evaluation Report Form B-91. Syracuse, N.Y.: Bardeen's Inc. (not dated).

Terman, Louis M. and Maud A. Merrill. *Revised Stanford-Binet Scores*. Boston: Houghton Mifflin Company (1937).

Thompkins, E. and V. Roe. *The Case for and Against Merit Rating: Digest of Significant References*, 1951-1956. Washington, D. C.: Association of Secondary School Principals (June 1, 1956).

Thurstone, L. L. and Thelma Gwinn Thurstone. *SRA Primary Mental Ability Tests*. Chicago: Science Research Associates (1949).

Toops, Herbert A. *Ohio State University Psychological Test*. Columbia Ohio College Association, Ohio State University (1950).

Turner, R. L. "Problem Solving Proficiency Among Elementary School Teachers." Bloomington, Indiana: Institute of Educational Research, Indiana University (1964).

Turner, R. L. and N. A. Fattu. "Skill in Teaching: A Reappraisal of the Concepts and Strategies in Teacher Effectiveness Research." *Bulletin of School of Education*. Indiana University (1960).

Utah School Merit Study Committee, Salt Lake City, 223 State Capitol, *Report and Recommendations*, Utah School Merit Study (1958), *passim*.

Vander Werf, Lester S. "Education for Teaching," *Journal of Teacher Education*, V, No. 4. (December, 1954), 288-291.

————."The Evaluation of Teaching," *American School Board Journal*, CXXXIII, No. 4 (October, 1956), 27-30.

————. *How to Evaluate Teachers and Teaching*. New York: Rinehart and Company (1958), *passim*.

————, and Vincent J. Glennon. *The Modern Classroom Guide*. Boston: Clark-Franklin Press (1955).

Vasche, Joseph Burton. "How Well Do You Teach?" *Journal of NEA*, XXXV, No. 6 (September, 1946), 293-294.

Wandt, Edwin and Leonard M. Ostreicher. "Variability in Observing Classroom Behavior of Junior High School Teachers and Classes." New York: Division of Teacher Education, Office of Research and Evaluation, College of the City of New York (June, 1953).

Watson, Goodwin, and E. M. Glaser. *Critical Thinking Appraisal*. Manual. Yonkers-On-Hudson, N.Y.: World Book Company (1952).

Wechsler, David. *Wechsler-Bellevue Intelligence Scale*. New York: Psychological Corporation (1947).

Wiles, K. *Supervision for Better Schools*, 2nd ed. New York: Prentice-Hall, Inc. (1955), Chs. XIII-XIV.

Wirtz, R. W. "Nonverbal Instruction." *The Arithmetic Teacher* (1963).

Woodring, P. *A Fourth of a Nation.* New York: McGraw-Hill (1959).

———. *New Directions in Teacher Education.* New York: The Fund for the Advancement of Education (1957), Ch. IV.

Wright, Moorhead. "Development of Men," address before American Association of Advertising Agencies, 38th Annual Meeting (1956).

Yeager, W. A. *Administration and the Teacher.* New York: Harper and Brothers (1954), Ch. XIV.

INDEX

Index